INDIAN VILLAGES
of the
SOUTHWEST

*A Practical Guide
to the Pueblo Indian Villages
of New Mexico and Arizona*

Buddy Mays

Chronicle Books · San Francisco

Library of Congress Cataloging in Publication Data

Mays, Buddy.
    Indian villages of the Southwest.

    Bibliography: p.
    Includes index.
    1. Pueblo Indians. 2. Pueblos—Southwest, New.
3. Southwest, New—Description and travel—1981—
Guide-books. I. Title.
E99.P9M37   1985   979   84-11331
ISBN 0-87701-735-2

10   9   8   7   6   5   4

Editing: Carey Charlesworth
Composition: Accent & Alphabet, Seattle

Chronicle Books
275 Fifth Street
San Francisco, California 94103

Contents

Acknowledgments

I am deeply grateful for the patience and assistance given me during production of this book by John O'Brien, Ruth Armstrong, Ken and Karen Hardy, Jerry Montgomery, and the Pueblo people of New Mexico and Arizona. I would also like to thank the Pueblo Indian Cultural Center in Albuquerque, New Mexico, and the Wheelwright Museum in Santa Fe for their help in obtaining photographs that would otherwise have been unavailable.

It is the tragedy of native American history that so much human effort has come to naught, and that so many hopeful experiments in life and in living were cut short by the devastating blight of the white man's arrival. There can be little doubt that had they [Pueblo Indians] been allowed to work out their own salvation, they would eventually have overcome their difficulties and might have built up a civilization of a sort not yet attempted by any group of men.

A. V. Kidder

Hopi woman making pottery
circa 1890s.

Note

Two pueblos are not included in this guidebook. Pojoaque Pueblo, north of Santa Fe, New Mexico, exists in name only and has virtually ceased to function as a community. Santa Ana Pueblo, west of Bernalillo, New Mexico, is still inhabited but allows entry by non-Indians only one day a year.

For My Mother

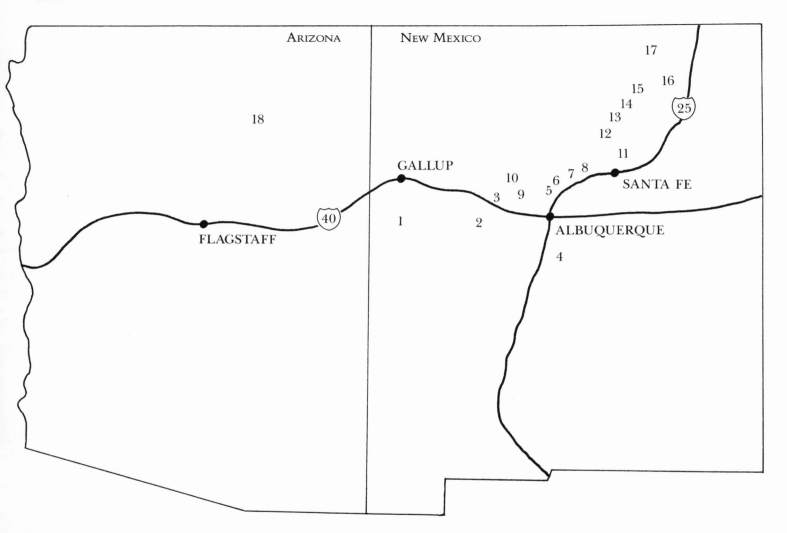

Pueblos Of The Southwest

1. Zuni
2. Ácoma
3. Laguna
4. Isleta

5. Sandía
6. San Felipe
7. Santo Domingo
8. Cóchiti

9. Zia
10. Jemez
11. Nambé
12. Tesuque

13. San Ildefonso
14. Santa Clara
15. San Juan
16. Picurís

17. Taos
18. Hopi

Introduction

W HEN the first Spanish expedition arrived in the Southwest in 1540 A.D. it found the region inhabited by a large number of native people. Most of these aborigines were concentrated in what the conquistadors called pueblos—compact, multi-storied towns of from 50 to 800 rooms, usually built around a central square or plaza. Modern historians estimate that 80 to 100 occupied pueblos, housing between 20,000 and 30,000 Indians, existed in the Southwest when the Spanish rode into the region.

A peaceful, submissive people were these pueblo folk, and prim-itive possibly, but hardly savages. Their economic base was agricul-ture, and most of the larger towns were girdled by carefully tended fields of cotton, tobacco, corn, beans, and squash. Trade with Indian tribes from Mexico and the West Coast had been established for cen-turies, and the arts of pottery making, weaving, and jewelry production were highly developed. Four native tongues, somewhat delineating variations in a common culture, were spoken by the Indians: Tanoan (with Tiwa, Tewa, and Towa dialects), Zuni, Keresan, and Shoshonean. (For each pueblo in this book, the language spoken is noted under the appropriate section heading.) Though no written language existed, tribal lore and history were passed from generation to generation quite satisfactorily by word of mouth.

Of course, the pueblo people were not the first natives of the New World that the Spaniards had encountered. In 1521, Hernán Cor-tés—with only 500 men, 16 horses, and 30 thirty muskets—defeated the formidable Aztec empire and subsequently conquered all the Indi-ans of Mexico. During the next few years, thousands of Europeans—most of them seduced by visions of gold—set forth from Mexico City to explore and colonize whatever fragments of the New World they could reach. Quite often, natives who objected to the Spanish expan-sion were slaughtered.

One of the adventure-seeking young men was Pánfilo de Narváez, who in 1528, with 300 Spanish soldiers, landed on the coast of Florida in search of treasure. The expedition met with little resistance at first, but then on a trip inland Narváez ran into serious trouble. As one chronicler benignly put it, "the residents were hostile and amused themselves at cracking Spanish heads with war clubs." Badly outnumbered by angry, aggressive natives and unable to return to their ship, Narváez and his men fought their way to the nearest point of coastline. There, they killed their horses, constructed five leaky boats from the hides, and set sail westward, pursuing the coastline back to Mexico. Fate, however, was not kind to the Narváez expedition. Adrift for only a few days, the small flotilla was wrecked by a storm, and all but five of the Spaniards drowned. The survivors—among them Alvar Núñez, former treasurer of the expedition, and Estevancio, a former Moorish slave—somehow reached shore but were promptly captured by local Indians and sold into slavery. Six long years later a ragged quartet escaped to head west again (one man elected to stay with his captors), and after months of near starvation crossed the Río Grande and finally reached Mexico City and safety. Their hazardous journey was possibly the most amazing feat in the history of Spanish colonization.

In later reports to the government, Núñez claimed to have seen many signs of precious metal during his trip, and he proposed a treasure-hunting expedition north toward the Río Grande. Several years later the request was finally approved by Spanish officialdom, but command of the expedition was offered not to Núñez but to Francisco Vázquez de Coronado, the rowdy, adventurer son of a noble Spanish family who had come to Mexico seeking his fortune.

While Coronado gathered men and supplies for the trip, a smaller party, led by the former slave Estevancio and a missionary named Marcos de Niza, set forth to scout the proposed route. Weeks later, in the wilds of northern Mexico, Estevancio received reports from local Indians that ahead of them lay a cluster of towns built from pure gold—a tale suspiciously similar to an old Portuguese treasure legend that described seven golden cities in a land called Cíbola. Leaving Fray Marcos to push forward with the main party, Estevancio went on ahead with a handful of Indian porters, and a few weeks later he reached the Zuni village of Hawikuh, becoming the first European to do so. Claiming to be a medicine man, Estevancio made himself at home, demanding food and women from the Indians. When he was ordered to leave and didn't, Zuni warriors carved the former slave into little pieces (so say the legends) and cast his remains to the desert. Fray Marcos, upon learning of his companion's death, abandoned his quest temporarily and retraced his steps south to Mexico, there to join Coronado.

The main Coronado expedition—336 soldiers and priests, 599 horses, and several hundred Indian porters—reached Hawikuh in July 1540. As they approached the village Coronado sent runners ahead, requesting peace, but at the outskirts of Hawikuh the Spaniards were attacked. Coronado ordered a charge; the battle lasted an hour, ending when the Zunis fled. Hawikuh and five other nearby villages belonged to the soldiers.

The Spaniards found food and shelter in "Cíbola" but little else. Of Estevancio's seven golden cities there was no sign. Coronado occupied the Zuni region for nearly six months while exploration parties went east and west, then in December he moved on to the Río Grande. The expedition wintered in Tiguex, a cluster of 12 sizable pueblos situated near the site of present-day Albuquerque, New Mexico.

Partially restored houses at Ácoma.

Coronado was met with strained hospitality at Tiguex but no outright violence until soldiers began raping pueblo women and stripping the villages of food and clothing to meet their own needs. The Indians objected strenuously, and for several months a series of running battles took place both in and around the pueblos. Finally Coronado ordered the Tiguex villages to be burned to the ground, one by one. Hostilities ceased, mainly because the Indians, now homeless, had taken refuge in the hills. For the next year Coronado scouted the region thoroughly, going as far east as Kansas. No treasure, however, did he find. In 1542 the expedition returned, emptyhanded, to Mexico. Coronado later was brought to trial for his mistreatment of the Indians but was acquitted of all charges.

During the next four decades the Pueblo Indians were left entirely to themselves. Then, in 1581, the Spaniards came again. First to arrive was the Rodríguez-Chamuscado expedition—3 priests, 8 soldiers, and 19 friendly Indians—in search of souls to save. Two years later came Antonio de Espejo, like Coronado looking for gold. In 1590 Gaspar Castaño de Sosa, an aggressive, unscrupulous slave trader from northern Mexico, made the long trip up the Río Grande accompanied by 170 men, women, and children and a large herd of horses and cattle. Castaño's first goal was to establish a permanent settlement in the province now known as New Mexico; his second, to find treasure. In both cases he failed, but the rush toward the land of the Pueblo Indian had begun.

Juan de Oñate, first official governor of New Mexico, arrived in the province in 1598 with 270 soldiers and priests and nearly 7,000 head of livestock. Oñate established a settlement at the pueblo of O'ke (San Juan), constructed the first Catholic church in the region, and ordered that all Indians be converted to the faith. By 1630 Spanish priests resided in most major pueblos and, using forced Indian labor, had constructed a chain of missions. Traditional Indian religion in most cases had been banned, and use of the kiva—an underground chamber in which sacred Indian rites are held—had been outlawed.

Numerous atrocities, including beatings, mutilations, and even killings, occurred during this period. In addition, government officials imposed a system of agricultural taxation called La Encomienda

whereby pueblos were forced to tithe to the church and to various bureaucrats in the capital of Santa Fe. Indian agriculture suffered, and in some cases, especially in rainless years when harvests were small, there was near starvation. Then came the final blow. In 1675, 47 Indian religious leaders were arrested for bewitchment and murder. They were brought to trial in Santa Fe and pronounced guilty. Four were immediately hung in the plazas of their respective pueblos; the others received public floggings and harsh prison terms.

This false indictment of respected medicine men was the final straw. Covertly, tribal leaders from the major villages began to plot an uprising. On August 10, 1680, the revolt took place; in a coordinated surprise offensive, heavily armed warriors from each pueblo rose up against their Spanish masters, first killing those actually living in the villages, then moving into the countryside to attack the haciendas and small farms. In the first three days of fighting more than 400 Spanish men, women, and children died at the hands of the Indians, many of them mutilated beyond recognition. Twenty priests were killed as well. Most of the great adobe missions were burned to the ground.

A week later, contingents of warriors from each pueblo besieged Santa Fe. Inside the city's walls were Governor Antonio de Otermín

Left. Tribal elder at Santa Clara Pueblo.
Right. Child selling pottery at Ácoma.

and a thousand refugee Spaniards—the majority of them women and children. Under a white flag, Indian war chiefs notified the governor that he and the survivors of the Pueblo Revolt were free to leave New Mexico unharmed if they did so immediately; instead, Otermín and what few able-bodied soldiers remained launched an attack of their own. If Spanish documents can be believed, 300 Indians were killed in the battle and hundreds more put to flight. Then, without incident, Otermín and his entourage abandoned the capital and headed south to Isleta Pueblo (which did not take part in the Pueblo Revolt), where they joined ranks with 1,500 other refugees. When the few remaining supplies had been divided, the long, ragged line of defeated, half-starved Spaniards headed down the Río Grande toward El Paso. The Indians were free at last.

In the years that followed the Spaniards made several attempts to retake New Mexico, but none was successful. Otermín returned in 1681 accompanied by a small band of soldiers, but he retreated quickly when his scouts reported heavily armed warriors awaiting them north of Isleta. Two years later Otermín was replaced as chief executive and, in 1688, new governor Domingo Cruzate made a hit-and-run raid into the province, hoping to either reconquer New Mexico or at the very least sack a few pueblos. On August 29 he and his brigade of hand-picked men reached the Indian town of Zia and, without requesting surrender, immediately attacked. In the battle that followed, 600 pueblo inhabitants died and Zia was set ablaze. Cruzate returned to El Paso, his mission at least partially accomplished.

The official reconquest of the province began in 1692. At the order of Carlos II, king of Spain, conquistador Diego de Vargas and 200 men rode north from El Paso along the Río Grande and, on September 13, entered Santa Fe without firing a shot. From the Indians gathered there, de Vargas demanded and received an oath of obedience, promising very little in return. He was told by a war chief that the leaders of the Pueblo Revolt were dead and that, though he might expect trouble from a few belligerent villages, most would once again accept Christianity and Spanish rule.

The Spanish reentry into Santa Fe has been called the bloodless reconquest of New Mexico. It was not. During the next four years

Spanish soldiers fought numerous battles with renegade pueblos, killing hundreds, perhaps thousands of Indians in the process. De Vargas even had to retake Santa Fe by force a year later when the pueblo warriors there defaulted on their promise of obedience. By 1700, however, Spanish domination had been almost fully restored. New missions had been constructed, and a company of priests were once again busy saving souls. Settlers began arriving daily from Mexico, and farming villages sprang up like wildflowers in the hills and valleys surrounding Santa Fe.

In the pueblos themselves, life continued much as it had before the Revolt — a difficult existence at best. In most cases the atrocities ceased but were quickly replaced by other hardships. Smallpox, a disease brought to the New World by the Spaniards, swept the pueblos, killing 5,000 Indians in a single year. Nomadic tribes of Plains Indians raided at will, forcing hundreds to abandon their traditional homes and move to the relative security of larger, more protected villages. This in turn brought about overpopulation and shortages of food and clothing. Unwanted religion was still being crammed down the Indians' throats by priests who had little or no concept of the people with whom they were dealing. And to make matters worse, political control of the pueblos changed hands on two separate occasions in the next 150 years — from Spain to Mexico in 1821, and from Mexico to the United States in 1846. With each change came a new list of regulations to which the Indians were forced to adhere and a new set of government officials to whom they had to answer.

These centuries of conflict, anger, frustration, and despair have taken a grave toll on the Indian pueblos of the Southwest. Today, only 29 of the original 80 to 100 still function as communities, and some anthropologists say that within 50 years pueblo life will cease altogether. Of the approximately 40,000 Pueblo Indians alive today, nearly a fourth have left the reservation permanently, to work and reside in the cities of the white man. No one, not even the most conservative tribal official, will deny that massive changes have occurred in pueblo life—the majority in the last 50 years—and that more will occur in the future. However, the binding force that has for centuries united Pueblo Indians everywhere—an unshakable, totally encompassing spiritual belief that life will somehow continue—is no less potent today than it was in the 16th, 17th, and 18th centuries. Will it be enough to prevent addition of the Pueblo Indian culture to the growing list of those that have been obliterated? Only time will tell.

Pueblo Etiquette

EACH Indian pueblo in New Mexico and Arizona, although basically similar to the others in outward physical appearance, is governed by its own group of tribal officials and consequently has its own set of rules and regulations. These are typically listed on signs at the pueblo entrances or described in brochures available at the local governor's offices. However some pueblos simply don't bother with this, and visitors are pretty much on their own. The following general rules are those you should follow when touring any reservation.

1. Don't be loud or obnoxious. Keep a low profile at all times, and remember that when you walk through an Indian village you're walking through someone's home, not a national park.

2. Don't take photographs in the pueblos that allow photography until you have purchased a photo permit, if required, or have obtained permission from the individual you wish to shoot, if a permit is not required. In the villages where photography is prohibited, don't even remove your camera from the car. If you do the possibility is excellent that, along with your film, it will be permanently confiscated. The same rules apply to tape recorders and sketch pads.

Indians who allow their pictures to be taken usually expect a small token of your gratitude—$1 to $3 depending upon the individual. Sure, you're buying the picture, but frankly you won't get it otherwise.

3. Obey all traffic signs in the pueblos and keep your speed at a crawl. Don't take photographs through car windows where picture taking is prohibited.

4. Keep off old buildings (they're dangerous), and stay well clear of restricted zones and kivas. Attempting to enter a kiva is a sure-fire way to end up in the tribal jail.

5. Almost all Pueblo Indians speak English in addition to their native tongue and many speak Spanish as well, so when around them don't talk as though they weren't there. And be polite. Whenever meeting a pueblo resident—man or woman—offer to shake hands. Call elders sir or ma'am (or mother or father), and don't be afraid to introduce yourself.

If by chance you run across an Indian who does not speak English, gesture, smile, and point if you want something. You'll be surprised at the results. Pueblo Indians were using sign language long before the white man appeared.

6. If you run into hostility from a tribal official, don't worry about it. Usually the pueblo residents are far nicer. However, don't expect most village inhabitants to bend over backwards for you. Exactly the opposite is usually the case. The fact is, most Indians associate with tourists only because of their dollars.

7. When dealing with vendors, don't accept the first price asked for any item. Bargain a bit; it's what most vendors expect.

8. Be patient. Indian ways are not white man's ways, and no matter how inconvenienced you might be, you won't be able to change things by getting angry.

9. Don't offer an Indian liquor of any type. Not only is it against the law but it's a big step toward discovering that Indians don't make pleasant drunks.

10. When attending dances or ceremonies, keep clear of the performers. Don't walk across the dance plaza, and don't sit or stand in front of pueblo residents.

11. Place all trash in proper receptacles even if you see Indians throwing it on the ground. They're entitled; you're not. In areas such as Taos and Picuris where a stream or lake is nearby, don't enter the water or throw anything in it. You could be polluting the pueblo's drinking water.

Buffalo dancers at Santa Clara Pueblo.

The Pueblo of Ácoma

K E R E S A N

ORIGINAL INDIAN NAME   Ákome— "People of the White Rock."

HOW TO GET THERE   From Albuquerque, drive west on Interstate 40 to the junction of N.M. 23 (exit 108), about 45 miles. Turn left on N.M. 23 and follow it to the pueblo entrance, 12 miles south.

ELEVATION   6,600 feet

HOURS   7 A.M. to 5 P.M. daily except during closed religious ceremonies, which may occur at any time. To make sure the pueblo is open, call the Ácoma Governor's Office shortly before your visit.

ADMISSION   Adults, $3; children under 16, $1.50; children under 12, $1. Mesa-top parking is $.50 per car. (You can park at the bottom for free and walk up, if you wish.) Admission and parking fees should be paid at the Ácoma registration office atop the mesa.

PHOTOGRAPHY   Yes: $3 for each still camera; $10 for each movie camera or video recorder. Sketching permits cost $30. Photographs of the Ácoma cemetery or the interior of San Esteban Rey Mission are prohibited.

San Isteban Rey Mission at Ácoma.

PERCHED atop a dramatic 365-foot-high, slab-sided sandstone mesa, Ácoma is appropriately called the Sky City. Probably built around 900 A.D., it is one of the oldest occupied villages in the United States.

The pueblo's initial contact with Europeans came in 1541 when Capt. Hernándo de Alvarado and 20 Spanish soldiers stopped at the lofty village to demand supplies. Alvarado later wrote to his commander-in-chief, Francisco Coronado, that the pueblo

> is one of the strongest ever seen, because the city is built upon a very high rock. The ascent was so difficult that we repented climbing to the top. The houses are three to four storeys high. The people are of the same type as those in the province of Cíbola [Zuni], and they have abundant supplies of maize, beans, and turkeys like those of New Spain [Mexico].

Alvarado also reported that the village contained an estimated population of 6,000 and that the mesa's only access was a narrow path literally carved from solid rock.

For the next half century Ácoma was left alone by all save a few priests. Then in 1598 Juan de Oñate, newly appointed governor of New Mexico, toured the pueblo. Later that same year Oñate's nephew, Juan de Zaldívar, was sent to demand tribute and supplies. Fed up with Spanish extortion, Ácoma warriors attacked, and in a short, ferocious battle Zaldívar and 13 of his soldiers were killed. The survivors quickly retreated.

On January 12, 1599, Zaldívar's brother, Vicente, returned to the pueblo accompanied by 70 heavily armed men and demanded that the Indians responsible for the attack surrender. When no answer was forthcoming, Zaldívar placed the pueblo under siege and with a handful of men fought his way to the mesa top. Three days later, 800 Indians had been killed without a single Spanish loss. The Sky City

INTERPRETIVE SERVICES   All visitors to the pueblo are accompanied by Indian guides. Tours leave every half hour from the registration office; they are about ¾ mile in length and require an hour and a half. The cost of the guide is included in the admission fee.

Brochures about Ácoma Pueblo are available at the registration office. A new tribal museum has been under construction and should be open by 1984. Tribal officials say it will house a large collection of Ácoma artifacts dating back 800 years.

ARTS AND CRAFTS   Ácoma artisans are best known for their black-on-white and black-and-red-on-white pottery. Most of the better ware is handmade in the village, then fired in traditional firing pits in the valley below, using cow dung as fuel. Ácoma pottery, usually elaborately decorated with angular and curvilinear geometric designs, ranks among the most beautiful of all pueblo ceramics.

Little Chief Trading Post—at the base of Ácoma Mesa—has a small selection of pottery for sale, but the best quality ware is usually sold privately from pueblo homes. If you're interested, ask your tour guide. However, if small souvenirs are more to your taste, a number of "tabletop" salesmen located at strategic points along the pueblo's streets offer a wide selection of small, inexpensive "tourist pots" (gaudily painted bowls and vases that have not been archivally fired).

was burned, and 600 captives were transported under guard to Santo Domingo pueblo near the Río Grande, to stand trial. The verdict: Guilty! All Ácoma men over 25 years of age were sentenced to 20 years in prison and the amputation of one foot. Elderly men and women were sold to friendly Plains Indians as slaves. Only children under 12 were released without punishment.

About 1603 Ácoma was rebuilt by surviving tribal members. A huge mission was constructed in 1629, using forced Indian labor under the dictatorial command of Spanish priests. When the pueblos revolted in 1680 the great mission was destroyed and the residing priest, Fray Lucas Maldonado, murdered. Not until 1699, long after most other pueblos had surrendered to the Spanish reconquest, did Ácoma finally capitulate and allow the priests to return and the mission to be rebuilt.

Today, Ácoma is one of the friendliest and most primitive of all the Southwestern pueblos. Although several reconstruction projects are currently underway (mainly for the sake of safety), visitors can still view many of the original two- and three-story dwellings. By tribal consensus, few modern conveniences have been allowed. Village residents still carry drinking water from natural stone catch basins that have served as cisterns for a thousand years. The few television sets and radios in the pueblo operate only on batteries. All heating and cooking is done with wood.

The massive San Esteban Rey Mission still stands on its original construction site. Mud and brick walls of the church are 9 feet thick, and the roof beams are 40 feet in length. The latter, each weighing several hundred pounds, were hand-carried from 11,000-foot-high Mount Taylor, more than 40 miles away. (Legends say that, in transit, the logs were never allowed to touch the ground.) Every bit of material used in the mission's construction, in fact, including the dirt in an adjoining 2,000-square-foot cemetery, was brought to the mesa top by hand from elsewhere.

Inside the church, though not on public display, is a large painting of Saint Joseph, presented to the pueblo sometime during the first part of the 17th century. This ancient piece of Spanish art was responsible for one of the greatest controversies in pueblo history (as discussed in the entry *The Pueblo of Laguna*) and is perhaps the most

PUBLIC CEREMONIES   Only three celebrations are always held on the same days each year at Ácoma— Saint Lawrence Day on August 10; Feast Day, dedicated to Saint Stephan, on September 2; and Christmas festivities, on December 24. All three celebrations are accompanied by Indian dances.

Various other fiestas and religious events occur throughout the year, but dates for these are seldom fixed. For up-to-date information, call the governor's office the month before your visit.

Cameras, tape recorders, and sketch pads are prohibited at all public ceremonies. Pueblo officials enforce this regulation heartily.

VISITOR FACILITIES   Camping and picnicking facilities are available at Acomita Lake Recreation Site, situated 10 miles north of the pueblo on Indian Road 38. Permits cost $4 per day per car. The lake contains both catfish and trout, and the fishing season runs from March 1 through December 15. Permits cost $2.75 per day for adults and $1.50 per day for children under 10; they may be purchased at the lake. A New Mexico license also is required. Boating and swimming are prohibited. A snack bar, a bait shop, and restrooms are located near the campground.

Telephone (505) 552-6604

Ácoma potter.

prized Spanish artifact in any New Mexico pueblo.

The Ácoma reservation consists of 262,000 acres. Total tribal population is slightly more than 3,000, but only 10 or 15 families reside permanently in the old village. The rest, probably because they like modern conveniences as well as anyone, live either in the nearby town of Acomita or in a new Housing and Urban Development (HUD) division near Interstate 40 on the reservation's northern boundary. Though a few Ácoma residents hold jobs in Grants and Albuquerque, most are stockmen, farmers, or are involved in the arts and crafts industry.

The Pueblo of Cóchiti

ORIGINAL INDIAN NAME   Kotyete— "Stone Kiva."

HOW TO GET THERE   From Albuquerque drive north on Interstate 25 about 40 miles and turn left on N.M. 16. At the junction of N.M. 22, turn right and follow the signs to the pueblo entrance.

ELEVATION   5,300 feet.

HOURS   8 A.M. to 5 P.M. daily, except during religious ceremonies.

ADMISSION   Free. Tribal leaders ask only that you obtain permission to visit the pueblo from the governor's office.

PHOTOGRAPHY   No; photographs are strictly prohibited. Cameras, recording devices, and sketch pads found in the village will be confiscated.

INTERPRETIVE SERVICES   None. Visitors are allowed to wander through the pueblo unaccompanied but should steer clear of the well-marked restricted areas and kivas. No brochures are available.

The most famous of the "Story Teller" potters, Helen Cordero of Cóchiti.

LOCATED on the west bank of the Río Grande, this small Keresan pueblo has occupied the same site since about 1250 A.D. Archaeological evidence suggests that Cóchiti ancestors once inhabited the ancient Anasazi town of Tyuonyi, one of several abandoned villages in the Jemez Mountains to the west. A harsh drought in the early 13th century probably drove the Tyuonyi inhabitants to the river valley, where a permanent source of water existed in the Río Grande.

The first European to visit the pueblo was Fray Agustín Rodríguez, a Spanish priest in search of Christian converts who reached the Río Grande Valley in 1581. Rodríguez was murdered by warriors from another pueblo shortly thereafter, and for 10 years Cóchiti was left to itself. In 1591, would-be-colonizer-of-New-Mexico Gaspar Castaño de Sosa stopped at the village for supplies. Castaño remained only a few days, but other Spaniards, hundreds of them, were not long in coming.

The Mission of San Buenaventura ("Saint of Good Fortune") was built probably between 1625 and 1630. (Exact construction dates have been lost.) During the Pueblo Revolt of 1680, the great church was burned. Legend says the resident priest escaped with his life only because he disguised himself as an Indian and slipped from the pueblo under cover of darkness.

Following the uprising, the inhabitants of Cóchiti abandoned their village and took refuge—along with Indians from nearby Santo Domingo Pueblo—in a mountain stronghold called Cieneguilla until all threat of Spanish reprisal had passed. In 1692, when Diego de Vargas began the reconquest of New Mexico, once again the Cóchiti people fled to Cieneguilla. A year later de Vargas placed the Indian stronghold under siege, and, when the battle was over, 20 warriors had been killed and 300 women and children captured. Most were allowed to return to their village not long afterward, to help in construction of a new

ARTS AND CRAFTS   Cóchiti artisans are well known for horsehide drums, turquoise jewelry, and black-on-cream pottery. Perhaps the most unique creation from the pueblo is the Cóchiti "storyteller pottery"—clay figurines of people and animals in lifelike situations. Storytelling with ceramics is a recent pueblo innovation, begun in the 1960s, and has little to do with Cóchiti tradition.

Trading posts or tourist shops do not exist here. Arts and crafts are sold either at local Indian fairs or by private vendors from their homes. A small sign, usually placed in the window or nailed to a tree in the yard, indicates an artisan in residence.

PUBLIC CEREMONIES   Dances and religious ceremonies occur throughout the year at the pueblo, but many are restricted to tribal members only. Those of interest to visitors are San Antonio's Day and San Juan's Day, both held in June (dates vary) and both accompanied by dances, and the Cóchiti Feast Day and corn dance, held July 14. Often, but not always, ceremonies occur during Christmas and New Year's holidays. For exact dates of all but Feast Day, call the pueblo before your visit.

Cóchiti woman carrying wood.

VISITOR FACILITIES   Overnight camping is allowed at a small, rustic campground located near the outlet of Cóchiti Lake (which you'll pass on the way to the pueblo). No hookups or restrooms. Camping permits cost $2 per night.

The tribe also operates a small fishing concession on the Rio Grande, in the stilling basin just below Cóchiti Dam. The river contains both trout and catfish. Permits cost $2 per person, and no state license is required. Both fishing and camping permits can be purchased from the Indian fish and game warden, who is usually parked from sunrise to sunset at the stilling basin.

Additional camping, fishing, picnicking, and boating are available at nearby Cóchiti Lake Recreation Area, located a few miles north of the pueblo on N.M. 22. This 1,200-acre reservoir offers marina facilities, a grocery store, restrooms, drinking water, and two large campgrounds with RV hookups.

Telephone (505) 465-2255

mission (still standing today). The few that did not return—diehards from Cóchiti and Santo Domingo both—escaped to the western portion of New Mexico, there to found Laguna Pueblo in 1699.

Today Cóchiti is in the throes of transformation. A few of the original structures still occupy traditional space around the central plaza, kiva, and church, but most of the pueblo's 800 tribal members reside in new, modern homes scattered from one end of the 28,000-acre reservation to the other. Less than a decade ago, most adults tended farms in the nearby river valley or raised stock in the mountainous foothills to the west; today, state and federal government jobs in Santa Fe and Albuquerque have enticed many to abandon agricultural pursuits and join a better-paying but faster-paced commuter economy. The village government is controlled by a conservative faction of tribal leaders who care little about tourists, and consequently the pueblo is far less cordial to non-Indian outsiders than it once was. As a result, tourism—once a major livelihood for many at Cóchiti—has suffered dramatically.

The pueblo is worth a visit nonetheless. Probably the most interesting of the few village attractions is the San Buenaventura Mission, located on the east side of the plaza. One hundred feet in length and 34 feet wide, it is filled with ancient statuary and paintings of French, Spanish, and Mexican workmanship. Much reconstruction has taken place in the past few years, but the structure is still an excellent example of post-Coronado mission architecture.

A typical "Story Teller" from Cóchiti.

The Pueblos of the Hopi

ORIGINAL INDIAN NAME   Hopituh— "Peaceful Ones."

HOW TO GET THERE   From Flagstaff, Arizona, drive 67 miles north on U.S. 89, and turn right on U.S. 160. At Tuba City, Arizona, turn right again on State Road 264. The Pueblo of Moenkopi is 3 miles farther; Third Mesa (Hótevilla, Bácobi, Oraibi) is 49 miles; Second Mesa (Shungopovi, Mishongnovi, Shipaúlovi) is 59 miles; First Mesa (Walpi, Hano, Sichomovi) is 75 miles. The entrance roads to all pueblos are plainly marked.

Alternate Route: From Gallup, New Mexico, drive north on U.S. 666 to the junction of State Road 264, about 7 miles, Turn left. First Mesa is 70 miles farther; Second Mesa is 86 miles; Third Mesa is 96 miles; Moenkopi is 142 miles.

ELEVATION   6,000 to 7,000 feet.

HOURS   9 A.M. to 6 P.M. daily (except during religious ceremonies) for all pueblos except Oraibi, which closes one hour earlier.

The Hopi pueblo Walpi on First Mesa circa 1880s.

TRIBAL myths and legends concerning Hopi origins are complex and extremely detailed. Basically they tell of how the first Hopi were created by Spider Woman in the Underworld, then sent through the Place of Emergence to reproduce and inhabit the earth. After many trials by fire and journeys to the four corners of the earth, the Hopi settled in their present location. Archaeologists suggest that the first Hopi town of Oraibi was constructed between 1020 and 1100 A.D., but that the desert region surrounding the village had been occupied for centuries. The other Hopi villages were constructed in the 17th and 18th centuries.

The Hopi's initial contact with Europeans occurred in 1540 when one of Coronado's soldiers—Capt. Pedro de Tovar—arrived at the town of Awátobi, demanding an oath of allegiance to God and the Spanish king. When the Indians refused, Tovar—with only 17 men—attacked. Overwhelmed (or at least surprised) by the Spaniard's weaponry, the Hopi people retreated and sued for peace. Tovar later wrote that Tusayan, as the Spanish called the Hopi region, contained seven main villages—Awátobi, Kawaiokuh, Walpi, Shipaúlovi, Shungopovi, Mishongnovi, and Oraibi. (All but Oraibi have since been destroyed or moved to new locations.) He estimated Tusayan's total population at 3,500.

After Coronado and his soldiers returned to Mexico, the Hopi region was not again bothered by outsiders for 43 years. Then came Antonio de Espejo and, a few years later, Juan de Oñate. Both were treated with hospitality and were allowed to tour the pueblos freely. In 1629, however, Spanish priests constructed five missions at Hopi— San Bernardino de Awátobi, San Francisco de Oraibi, San Bartolomé de Shungopovi, San Buenaventura de Mishongnovi, and an unnamed church at Walpi—and with the priests' arrival the trouble began. Tribal religion was banned, and use of the traditional ceremonial kivas was prohibited. Worse, Indian farmers who could themselves barely

ADMISSION   Oraibi, $1.50; all others free. At Oraibi you should stop at the house of Stanley Bahnimtewa, village chief, to pay your visitor's fee. The Bahnimtewa home is located on the left side of the road near the pueblo entrance.

PHOTOGRAPHY   No; all photography in the villages has been prohibited for several years. Cameras, tape recorders, and sketch pads found at the Hopi pueblos will be confiscated.

INTERPRETIVE SERVICES   The Hopi Cultural Center, located on Second Mesa 3 miles west of Shungopovi Pueblo, displays an excellent collection of 800-year-old artifacts, early photographs of the pueblos, and examples of contemporary arts and crafts. There are also a restaurant, motel, and several arts and crafts shops at the center. Open 9 A.M. to 5 P.M. daily; fee, $2; no brochures available.

ARTS AND CRAFTS   In sheer quantity, no other Indian tribe can match the Hopi when it comes to arts and crafts production. Local artisans make pottery, silver jewelry and serving ware, baskets, weavings, paintings, and kachina dolls.

Hopi pottery is traditionally dark brown and red on a light brown slip. It is sturdily made and relatively inexpensive, though larger bowls may cost $300 and more. Silver work includes not only jewelry but silverware, bowls, combs, brushes, and other house-

survive on meager harvests from a barren and almost waterless landscape were ordered to surrender a good portion of their crops to the church. In 1680, when the Pueblo Revolt occurred, the Hopi took an active (perhaps gleeful) part. Four priests were killed (two of them thrown bodily from the mesa cliffs) and all the missions destroyed. Twelve years later, when Diego de Vargas reconquered the Southwest, the Spaniard asked for and received pledges of peace from the Hopi villages, then quietly left the Indians to themselves. From that time to this no Catholic church has ever again stood on the Hopi mesas.

Shortly after the Pueblo Revolt, most of the Hopi villages were abandoned, to be rebuilt in new locations after the reconquest. And though, probably out of self-preservation, most of the Indians pretended friendship toward the Spaniards, their hatred for these armed, bearded men on horseback was evident. The village of Awátobi for instance, one of the Hopi towns not abandoned, made the imprudent mistake of inviting the Spanish priests to return after the reconquest. Fearful of renewed Spanish domination, the other Hopi pueblos joined together and, during an Awátobi ceremony when most of the village population was underground in the kiva, they attacked. Seven hundred Awátobi residents, many of them women, died in the next few hours. The pueblo was destroyed by the attackers and was never allowed to be rebuilt.

In the following years, new villages—Hano, Moenkopi, Hótevilla, and Bácobi—were founded. Hano was constructed by refugee Tewa Indians from the Río Grande pueblos who were fleeing the Spanish reconquest; Moenkopi began as a satellite farming community belonging to Oraibi but shortly established its own government. Hótevilla and Bácobi were founded as the result of internal conflict between conservatives and liberals at Oraibi. The former wanted to live in the traditional way without outside interference; the latter wanted help from the American government, mainly in the schooling of Oraibi children. In the ensuing political and physical struggle, the conservatives lost and were evicted. They moved a few miles west and founded Hótevilla. Shortly thereafter a few of their number attempted to return to Oraibi, but they were turned away. With nowhere to go, this small group founded Bácobi.

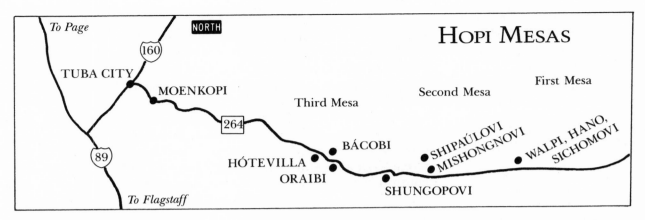

HOPI MESAS

To Page
NORTH
160
TUBA CITY
MOENKOPI
264
89
To Flagstaff

First Mesa
Second Mesa
Third Mesa
BÁCOBI
HÓTEVILLA
ORAIBI
SHUNGOPOVI
SHIPAÚLOVI
MISHONGNOVI
WALPI, HANO, SICHOMOVI

hold and personal items as well. Hopi baskets are made from Hilaria grass and yucca leaves, and they are in demand by tourists as well as by other Indian tribes. Weavings, produced by Hopi men (only rabbit-fur robes are woven by women), are made from locally raised sheep wool and usually colored with natural dyes.

Hopi kachina dolls, usually carved from the soft, dried roots of cottonwood trees and skillfully painted and decorated, represent Hopi spirits with great powers who from November to July join the world of mortal men. The sale of kachinas to non-Indians is relatively new with the Hopi; previously the dolls were thought too sacred to be allowed to leave the pueblos. Today, because of the heavy demand, they are expensive ($75 and up) but well worth the money as an investment.

Each Hopi village contains at least one "official" arts and crafts

Today there are nine mesa-top pueblos on the half-million-acre Hopi reservation, plus a number of newer, Americanized towns, scattered in the valleys below. About 5,500 Indians reside on the reservation, most of them artisans, stockmen, or farmers.

At first glance, the arid, desertlike landscape surrounding the Hopi mesa seems incapable of supporting a large, permanent population. The soil consists of sand and rock, and the average annual rainfall is seldom more than 12 inches. Summer temperatures can easily hit 120 degrees, and during the winter deep snow and subfreezing cold are common. Nonetheless, the Hopi have survived as an agricultural community here for at least 1,000 years. Somehow, sheep, goats, and cattle find enough to eat, foraging the sparse landscape in small herds and consuming everything from the tough "bunch" grass to spiny limbs of cholla cactus. Corn, bean, cotton, and melon fields, most less than an acre in size, are literally scraped from the sand and are planted not in rows but in clumps, so plants can be watered individually by hand if necessary. Seemingly the short growing season (slightly more than four months) combined with sandy soil and the deficient supply of water should create inadequate harvests. It should, but it doesn't; the Hopi thrive in this hostile environment, seldom if ever experiencing lean years.

The nine main Hopi villages, perched precariously on the fingerlike mesas that run north to south across the reservation, would make

shop, but most Hopi artisans prefer to sell their wares from private homes. Small signs tacked to fences or doorways indicate an artisan is in residence.

For a look at Hopi arts and crafts in production visit the Hopi Arts and Crafts Guild, located on Second Mesa just west of the Cultural Center. Tours of the facility are free.

PUBLIC CEREMONIES Kachina, flute, and snake and other animal dances occur at Hopi during every month except October. Most, but not all, are open to the public; for exact dates and locations, call the pueblos before your visit.

The Hopi religious year begins in November with the Naacnaiya and Wuwutcimti ceremonies, both marking the appearance of the kachinas from their traditional spirit homes on the San Francisco Peaks to the southwest. Other kachina dances—celebrating winter solstice, bean planting, requests for rain, and buffalo hunting—occur until July. The kachina dances end with the Niman Kachina Ceremony, which marks the return of the spirits to their Nuvatikiobi ("snow houses") on the San Francisco Peaks.

most architects shudder. Constructed mainly of shaped sandstone blocks bound together with only a minimum of mortar, the structures lean this way and that almost mindless of gravity. Walpi and Oraibi especially have changed very little since the time of the Spanish. Like a mist, an aura of oldness hangs over these two pueblos; visiting them is like walking through the pages of a history book.

Although a Hopi Tribal Council exists, each village elects its own chief, and it is he, not the council, who dictates pueblo policy. In one thing, however, the Hopi are together; they are perhaps the most religious of all Southwestern tribes. Daily life is permeated with and controlled by the kachinas—spirit ancestors of the Hopi people who intercede with the gods on the Indians' behalf. The large number of dances and other religious ceremonies held each year at the Hopi pueblos are not for the tourists alone; they are Indian prayers to the gods to ensure a productive and fruitful future.

Almost all of the Hopi villages are extremely friendly to outsiders. In the towns of Shungopovi, Mishongnovi, and Shipaúlovi on Second Mesa and Walpi and Sichomovi on First Mesa, an unofficial but very noticeable open-door policy exists, at least during the warmer months. Doors literally stand open during daylight hours, and those who knock will usually be greeted with a loud "Come in!" instead of the normal "Who is it?" Only Hótevilla and Bácobi still show signs of hostility toward outsiders. Frankly, neither is worth a visit except on dance days.

Hopi crafts.

Snake, antelope, butterfly, and flute dances begin about mid-August and end in September. The snake dance, one of the most dramatic of all Indian ceremonies, consists of pueblo priests dancing with reptiles (about a third of them rattlesnakes) in their mouths and is intended to bring rain and an abundant harvest. According to Hopi legends, no snake priest has ever died from snakebite—a mystery that has baffled anthropologists and herpetologists for decades.

Hopi officials request that all visitors who attend the dances dress properly—meaning fully clothed and wearing shoes. Don't attempt to covertly photograph or record the ceremonies; tribal officials are unforgiving if you're caught.

VISITOR FACILITIES   Overnight camping is not allowed at Hopi. Picnickers, on the other hand, are seldom bothered if they wish to use a roadside pullout while eating lunch. Motel accommodations are available at the Hopi Cultural Center on Second Mesa, as well as in Tuba City, Flagstaff, Keams Canyon, and Gallup.

Telephone
First Mesa: (602) 734-2262
Second Mesa: (602) 737-2570
Third Mesa: (602) 734-2404

Mishongnovi man circa 1880s.

The Pueblo of Isleta

ORIGINAL INDIAN NAME   Taug-weaga— "Kick-Flaking Stone Place People."

HOW TO GET THERE   From Albuquerque, take Interstate 25 south 14 miles to exit 209, leave the freeway, and turn left. Go about a mile, turn right on N.M. 45, and then turn immediately left onto U.S. 85. Follow the signs to the pueblo entrance, about a mile on the right.

ELEVATION   4,900 feet.

HOURS   8 A.M. to 5 P.M. daily, except during closed religious ceremonies.

ADMISSION   Free; permission is not needed to tour the pueblo.

PHOTOGRAPHY   Yes. Permits are not required to photograph the village or the church, but you should ask before taking pictures of individual Indians. A fee of $2 or $3 may be requested for the privilege.

INTERPRETIVE SERVICES   There is no museum. An informative booklet, *Isleta Pueblo and the Church of St. Augustine*, is available inside the church and gives an excellent history of the pueblo.

Saint Augustine Mission at Isleta.

THE people of Isleta claim their ancestors came from the mountains to the east of the Río Grande (the Manzano Mountains). The present village site was probably occupied sometime between 1200 and 1250 A.D.

In 1540 the pueblo was visited briefly by Capt. Hernando de Alvarado—a soldier in Coronado's expedition—but not until 1581 did the Indians have any lengthy contact with Europeans. Fray Agustín Rodríguez, a Spanish priest who stayed at Isleta during that year, later wrote that the village housed a population of 1,500 and contained 123 two- and three-story apartment houses.

The first mission was constructed at Isleta in 1613, and for the next 60 years the pueblo served as refuge both for Spanish settlers and other Indians who had been driven from their homes by Apache and Comanche raiders. When the Pueblo Revolt took place in 1680, Isleta did not participate—perhaps because of friendliness toward the Spanish but more likely because of a large Spanish garrison in the village. Whatever the reason, Isleta once again served as refuge—it was here that Governor Antonio de Otermín and his band of survivors came when they were forced out of Santa Fe a few days after the Revolt began.

A year after the uprising a 250-man expedition force, led by Governor Otermín, returned to New Mexico with hopes of retaking the province. At Isleta they found the mission partially destroyed and the main body of the structure being used as an animal pen. While the soldiers rested at the pueblo, scouts went north along the Río Grande. When they returned, the news they brought was bad; nothing but hostility awaited Otermín if he went north. A few weeks later the expedition returned to El Paso, unsuccessful in its reconciliation attempt, and with it went 385 Isleta Indians whom Otermín had taken prisoner. Later the captives were converted to Christianity, given land

ARTS AND CRAFTS   Probably the best known of all Isleta arts is its Indian breadbaking; loaves are baked daily in small beehive-shaped mud ovens called *hornos* and sold to visitors for about $2 a loaf. The pueblo's most famous baker is Felicita Jojola, who lives in a small house just east of the church. Early each morning Mrs. Jojola or a member of her family heats the hornos by burning a large pile of firewood stacked inside. When the fires have burned themselves out, coals are removed with a shovel and the ovens are swept clean. The loaves—usually about 50 of them—are placed on the still-hot floor and a wooden board is placed over the entrance to retain the heat. Usually the baking process takes about an hour; the result is a golden brown loaf, hot, crispy, and delicious. If you want to watch, be at the Jojola residence no later than 7:30 A.M.

Isleta artisans also produce pottery and turquoise and silver jewelry, none of it traditional. The pottery design is from Laguna Pueblo, usually red and black on white. The jewelry is copied from the Navajo.

Several Indian-owned shops where visitors may purchase local arts and crafts are found near the village. Among them are Margaret's Curios and Indian Jewelry, located 1 mile north of Isleta on U.S. 85; Isleta Village Jewelry, at the junction of U.S. 85 and N.M. 45; and the Isleta Pueblo Indian

along the river near El Paso, and instructed to build a new pueblo. They called the village Isleta del Sur.

When Diego de Vargas reconquered New Mexico in 1692, Isleta lay in ruins, probably burned by hostile pueblo tribes. Twenty years later the village was resettled by 300 Indians from Isleta del Sur and other Tiwa villages along the upper Río Grande. The great mission was rebuilt in 1720 and dedicated to Saint Augustine. (The first mission's patron saint had been Saint Anthony.)

Today Isleta is a friendly, prosperous town of 3,000 and is the largest of all New Mexico pueblos. (In tribal land holdings it ranks fourth with 211,000 acres.) Many of the original houses still stand around the large central plaza, although new paint, stucco, and television antennas have removed much of the traditional charm. A few Isletans still tend small farms in the river *bosque* ("bottomland"), but because of better wages a large majority of the adult population works in nearby Albuquerque and Belen.

Market Center, a large indoor crafts market adjacent to tribal headquarters.

PUBLIC CEREMONIES Dances and other religious ceremonies are held in January, April, August, September, and during the Christmas period. Dates and times vary, however; visitors should call the pueblo before their visits. Isleta Feast Day, dedicated to Saint Augustine and accompanied by a harvest dance, is held annually on September 4. Cameras, tape recorders and sketch pads are strictly prohibited during all religious ceremonies.

VISITOR FACILITIES Sunrise Lake, an Indian-owned-and-operated recreation area 3 miles northeast of the pueblo on N.M. 47, offers overnight camping, fishing, and picnicking. RV hookups cost $6 per night; tent camping, $4.50; fishing, $2.75. Camping and fishing permits can be purchased at the Isleta Tribal Store near the lake. Restrooms and drinking water are available at the campground; the lake contains trout and catfish, and no license is required.

Telephone (505) 869-3111

Left. Isleta women baking bread.
Right. Isleta pottery.
Far right. Isleta woman circa 1920.

The mission of Saint Augustine—entirely dominating the north end of the town plaza—lays claim to being the oldest church in New Mexico. It also offers one of the strangest ghost stories ever told. In 1756, a Spanish priest named Juan José Padilla died of an unknown illness at the pueblo and was buried in a wooden coffin beneath the church altar. Seventy years later, resident priests at Saint Augustine suddenly discovered that Fray Padilla and his coffin had literally popped up; both had risen from the grave and were showing clearly in the dirt floor. An examination of the body revealed another mysterious fact—it was virtually intact and displayed little sign of deterioration. The priest was rapidly reburied, but not before word got around that Fray Padilla's ghost—tired of the grave—had taken a stroll around the Isleta plaza, searching for sinners.

In a few years the rising of the priest was forgotten, but in 1889 up he came again. Again he was reburied. When Padilla showed up once more in 1962 (an eyewitness claims the body was still perfectly preserved), church officials decided he had frightened his last Catholic. This time the body was reburied beneath a 6-inch slab of concrete. Isleta Indians swear Fray Padilla is keeping an eye on them, but the official explanation for the Movable Priest is a variable water table beneath the church that floats the coffin upward during extremely wet years.

The Pueblo of Jemez

ORIGINAL INDIAN NAME   Walatow—"People in the Canyon."

HOW TO GET THERE   From Albuquerque drive 18 miles north on Interstate 25 to Bernalillo and turn left on N.M. 44 (exit 242). Go 23 miles to the junction of N.M. 4 and turn right. The pueblo is to the left 5 miles.

ELEVATION   6,000 feet.

HOURS   9 A.M. to 5 P.M. daily. Tribal offices are closed on weekends.

ADMISSION   Free. Visitors are requested to obtain permission from the Jemez Governor's Office if they plan a walking tour through the pueblo.

PHOTOGRAPHY   Photographs are allowed of the San Diego Mission only. No permit is required.

INTERPRETIVE SERVICES   None at the pueblo itself. Jemez State Monument (with the ruins of Gyusiwa Pueblo and the original San Diego Mission), located 20 miles north of Jemez Pueblo on N.M. 4, has a small museum that displays a col-

Jemez husband and wife in ceremonial dress.

JEMEZ legends claim the tribal ancestors originated in a great lagoon far to the north called Uabunatota. The people drifted slowly southward, say the old stories, until they found a secure home in the canyons of the Jemez Mountains.

When Coronado's expedition arrived in the Southwest, it discovered 10 Towa-speaking villages scattered in the foothills to the north of present-day Jemez. The first conquistador to visit these pueblos was Capt. Francisco de Barrio-Nuevo, who in 1541 named the Jemez region Aguas Calientes ("Hot Waters") because of the hundreds of thermal springs that dot the area. Juan de Oñate revisited the Jemez villages in 1598 and promptly ordered the Indians' Christianization. Spanish priests were quick to arrive and carry out Oñate's wishes.

In the early 17th century, the Jemez people were convinced by the Spaniards to abandon the most remote villages and centralize in Astiolakwa, Gyusiwa, and Patoqua, the three largest pueblos. Spanish officials undoubtedly realized that while scattered the Indians could be dangerous, but, concentrated, they could be controlled. By 1622 missions had been constructed in all three pueblos, and Oñate's order of conversion for the Jemez people was rapidly being implemented. Priests claimed that, by 1622, more than 6,000 Indians had become sons and daughters of God.

Spanish domination did not set well with the Jemez, however. When the Pueblo Revolt occurred in 1680 all three pueblos participated, killing several Spanish settlers in the vicinity and sending a large force of warriors to Santa Fe. Twelve years later, when Diego de Vargas reconquered New Mexico, he found Astiolakwa, Gyusiwa, and Patoqua abandoned and their former inhabitants living in small, heavily fortified villages in the mountains. Promising peace, de Vargas induced the Indians to return to the three larger pueblos, but there the Jemez remained only a short while. In the following four years they

lection of Jemez artifacts. Trails through the monument are self-guided. Brochures are available upon request.

ARTS AND CRAFTS   Jemez artisans produce plaited willow baskets, silver and turquoise jewelry, and heavy so-called utility pottery. The latter is usually all red or black and red on white. It is created primarily for sale to tourists and is not of traditional Towan design.

Although the utility ware carries nontraditional patterns, one pueblo potter refuses to let original Jemez pottery designs be lost. Evelyn Vigil, whose ancestors originally came from Pecos Pueblo (an abandoned Towan village 25 miles east of Santa Fe), still makes pottery in the traditional manner. Using only natural colors in her ware, she paints ancient Jemez designs with yucca leaf brushes, as did her ancestors, and fires in the traditional "pit" method using cow dung for fuel. Mrs. Vigil's pots and bowls are expensive but well worth the cost if you can locate them.

A small selection of Jemez arts and crafts is offered by the Jemez Trading Post, on the west side of N.M. 4 at the north end of the pueblo. Most artisans, however, prefer to sell privately from their homes. Look for small "Pottery" or "Indian Jewelry" signs tacked to doors or fences.

Bell tower of the old San Diego de Jemez Mission.

revolted twice more, both times retreating to their mountain strongholds. De Vargas used force to restore order and, in a series of short, murderous battles, the Jemez were well bloodied. Finally, with many of their women and children being held captive in Santa Fe, the Indians capitulated. Leaving the mountains for the last time, they constructed a new town called Walatow in the river valley a day's walk south of Gyuwisa. It is here that present-day Jemez Pueblo still stands.

The Jemez reservation today encompasses 88,000 acres. The pueblo is a large, rambling town of low-slung adobe buildings, most of which surround a wide central plaza. A few of the 2,100 residents work at state or federal jobs in Albuquerque, but most adults still tend farms near the river, raise cattle or sheep, or are involved in the arts and crafts trade.

PUBLIC CEREMONIES   Public dances and other religious ceremonies are held at Jemez in January, April, June, August, November, and December. Visitors should call the pueblo well before their visits for exact dates and times.

Jemez Feast Day is held annually on November 12 and is accompanied by the harvest dance. In early August, descendants of Pecos Pueblo Indians (who migrated to Jemez in 1838) perform the Pecos bull dance, considered one of the most colorful of all pueblo dances. The buffalo dance is usually held on December 25. Cameras, tape recorders, and sketch pads are strictly prohibited at all Jemez religious ceremonies.

Woman weaving traditional towan willow baskets at Jemez.

VISITOR FACILITIES Jemez Pueblo operates two day-use-only fishing ponds at Holy Ghost Recreation Site, 19 miles north of San Ysidro (a village you'll pass on your way to the pueblo) on N.M. 44. Fees vary from year to year but usually are between $2 and $5 per day. Permits should be purchased at the San Ysidro store. The ponds contain trout and catfish; no license is required. Restrooms and drinking water are available.

Overnight camping is prohibited on the reservation, but camping sites are available in the Santa Fe National Forest, 25 miles north of the pueblo on N.M. 4. Motel accommodations are available in Bernalillo and Albuquerque.

Telephone (505) 834-7459

Tribal religion and the practice of ancient traditions still play an important role in daily pueblo life, but as a whole the Jemez people are progressive. Recently a new tribal headquarters and 45 modern new homes were constructed in the town, and future plans include a new arts and crafts market and an expansion of the presently limited big game hunting industry. Unfortunately, the remote location of the pueblo has always presented a major stumbling block to modernization—especially where telephone and electric services are concerned. Nonetheless, tribal officials, most of them well educated, are eager and determined to move the town into the 20th century.

The answer, most tribal leaders say, is tourism. However, at least presently, Jemez has little to offer visitors other than its arts and crafts. The San Diego Mission, constructed in the early 1700s, is not one of the most attractive structures in the pueblo, and most visitors pass it by in favor of the original San Diego de Jemez Mission, located at the abandoned village of Gyusiwa (in Jemez State Monument) 20 miles north. Destroyed in the Pueblo Revolt, the ancient mission building is 111 feet in length, with 8-foot-thick adobe walls and a bell tower that rises 42 feet above the altar. Surrounding the old church are the partially excavated ruins of Gyusiwa, the pueblo that was the principal town of the Jemez during the 17th century but was abandoned in 1696 when present-day Jemez Pueblo was constructed.

Jemez in early winter.

A Jemez potter displaying her work.

The Pueblo of Laguna

ORIGINAL INDIAN NAME   Kawaik—meaning unknown.

HOW TO GET THERE   From Albuquerque, drive west on Interstate 40 to exit 114, about 40 miles. Leave the freeway and follow the frontage road west about a mile to the pueblo entrance.

ELEVATION   5,800 feet.

HOURS   8 A.M. to 5 P.M., except during closed religious ceremonies.

ADMISSION   Free. Permission to walk in the village is not needed.

PHOTOGRAPHY   Yes. Permits are not required. Tribal officials suggest that you ask village residents before taking their pictures; a small tip may be in order. Photographs are not allowed inside the San José Mission.

INTERPRETIVE SERVICES   None; no brochures available.

A crumbling wall from a 300-year-old building in Laguna.

LAGUNA is the newest of all Southwestern pueblos, settled in 1699 by refugees from Cóchiti, Santo Domingo, and Zia pueblos who were fleeing from the Spanish reconquest of New Mexico. Many of the original Laguna founders were inhabitants of Cieneguilla, a mountain stronghold of the Keresan tribes that Diego de Vargas attacked and destroyed in 1694. Later other Indians, from Ácoma, Zuni, Sandía, Jemez, and the Hopi Mesas, also settled in Laguna, in effect making the pueblo a melting pot of Southwestern Indian culture. And since Laguna was visited by Spaniards almost from the day of its birth, Hispanic influence as well played a major role in defining its policies.

Modern Laguna consists of six villages—Seama, Mesita, Encinal, Old Laguna (the original pueblo), Paguate, and Paraje—all within a few miles of each other. Archaeologists suggest this satellite system—with Old Laguna at the hub—was instigated during the 18th century to house a rapidly growing population of refugees from other pueblos.

The mother village of Old Laguna consists of a small cluster of stone and adobe dwellings perched atop a mound overlooking the Río San José. Until a few years ago Laguna retained much of its traditional charm, but recently several dozen modern homes and an uncountable number of trailer houses have transformed the village into a metal and plastic monstrosity.

The most prominent and beautiful building in Old Laguna is the San José Mission, begun in 1699 and completed in 1701. Though it is not one of the oldest churches in existence, the interior is certainly one of the most spectacular. Great floor-to-ceiling religious murals decorate the sanctuary, and portions of the altar are embellished with traditional Indian symbols, the origins of many of which have been lost or forgotten. On the church walls are several paintings of Spanish genesis

ARTS AND CRAFTS Only a few Laguna artisans are still active. A small amount of Ácomalike pottery is produced, along with plaited yucca and willow baskets, woven belts, and embroidery. The pueblo contains no shops or trading posts in which visitors can purchase local arts and crafts. Most are sold either at Indian-sponsored fairs held throughout the summer in various locations or by shops in Albuquerque and Santa Fe.

that according to historians were probably ferried across the Mexican desert on muleback.

It was a religious painting, in fact, that embroiled the pueblo of Laguna in one of the greatest controversies in Indian history. About 1620 a large painting of Saint Joseph was presented to a New Mexico priest named Juan Ramírez by King Charles II of Spain. A few years later the priest gave the painting to the people of Ácoma Pueblo, who placed it inside the Mission of San Esteban Rey atop the Ácoma Mesa. During the following century the Ácoma Indians came to believe the painting held miraculous powers, and whenever problems arose in the pueblo it was the painting of Saint Joseph to which the Indians appealed first. By 1750 the painting's fame had spread throughout the Southwest and it was held in veneration by almost all Indian tribes.

In 1800 Laguna Pueblo, near Ácoma and suffering from drought and sickness, appealed to Ácoma for loan of Saint Joseph in hopes that the painting would bring good fortune. Ácoma agreed to relinquish the prize for a month. When the month was up, however, Laguna begged for another 30 days. When that month was up and still no painting, Ácoma threatened war. And there, for the next 50 years, the dilemma remained. Saint Joseph stayed in Laguna, always under heavy guard.

In 1852 an Ácoma priest advised tribal elders to take the matter to court. Years of bitter accusations and massive legal fees followed, but finally the court decreed that Saint Joseph must be returned to the original owners. Strangely enough, when a group of Ácoma warriors went to fetch the painting from Laguna, they found the ancient work of art leaning against a tree on the trail between the two pueblos. To this day the Ácoma people believe that when Saint Joseph heard of the judge's decision he set forth for home on his own. Interested visitors can see the painting by special request at the San Esteban Rey Mission on the Ácoma Mesa.

Laguna Pueblo as a whole consists of six small, independent villages; each holds its own annual Feast Day dedicated to its patron saint:

Seama Village: July 26 (Santa Ana)

Mesita Village: August 15 (Our Lady of Ascension)

Encinal Village: September 8 (Nativity of the Blessed Virgin)

Old Laguna: September 19 (San José)

Paguate Village: September 25 (Saint Elisabeth)

Paraje Village: October 17 (Saint Margaret-Mary)

All Laguna feast days are accompanied by Indian dances.

Christmas festivities are normally held in Old Laguna on December 24, but visitors should call to make sure before their visits. Cameras, tape recorders, and sketch pads are forbidden during all Laguna ceremonies.

VISITOR FACILITIES   None. Camping, fishing, and picnicking facilities are available at nearby Acomita Lake. (See Visitor Facilities, *The Pueblo of Ácoma*.)

Telephone (505) 552-6654

The Laguna reservation consists of 441,000 acres and hosts a population of about 6,000. Tribal lands, once thought to be useless desert, have relinquished fortunes in uranium, marble, and other minerals, and consequently Laguna is a relatively wealthy tribe. Mesita, easternmost satellite of Laguna, is the site of a 42,000-square-foot industrial complex, and light industries are in the planning stages at several other locations. A few Laguna residents still make a living at sheep and cattle ranching, but most adults work at either the uranium mills or the marble plant, both located on the reservation.

The San José Mission at Laguna.

The Pueblo of Nambé

ORIGINAL INDIAN NAME   Nambé— "Mound of Earth in the Corner."

HOW TO GET THERE   From Santa Fe, drive 15 miles north on U.S. 84–285 to the junction of N.M. 4 and turn right. Drive 3 miles east and turn right again at the Bureau of Reclamation sign for Nambé Falls. The pueblo entrance is about 2 miles farther.

ELEVATION   6,175 feet.

HOURS   8 A.M. to 5 P.M. daily.

ADMISSION   Free. If you're not taking pictures, permission is not required to visit Nambé.

PHOTOGRAPHY   Yes. Permits cost $3 for each still camera, $5 for each movie camera, and $10 per sketch pad. Permits should be purchased at the Nambé Governor's Office, in the Tribal Headquarters Building. Ask permission from individuals before taking their photographs; picture-taking near the kiva is forbidden.

INTERPRETIVE SERVICES   None; no brochures available.

Nambé chief in front of his childhood home.

NAMBÉ Pueblo has been inhabited since before 1300 A.D., but the exact year of its initial occupation is unknown. Tribal legends claim that prior to Spanish arrival the Nambé people—far more numerous then than now—lived in eight large villages in the hills surrounding the present pueblo site.

Nambé was visited by exploration parties from the Coronado expedition on several occasions between the years 1540 and 1543, but exact dates either were never recorded or have been lost. The first chronicled visit occurred in 1591, when would-be colonizer Gaspar Castaño de Sosa camped at the pueblo for an evening. In the village plaza Castaño and his men erected a large wooden cross, notifying the Indians that they were now part of the Spanish province of New Mexico and would be required to pay tribute to the king. Tribal legends say the cross was torn down immediately after Castaño's departure.

Early in the 17th century the Spaniards built a large mission at Nambé, but when the Pueblo Revolt took place in 1680 the church was destroyed and a resident priest, Fray Tomás de Torres, was murdered. In 1729, following the reconquest of the province by Diego de Vargas, another mission was constructed, and this one stood until early in the 20th century when it collapsed while undergoing repairs. The small church that stands today in the Nambé plaza was built in 1972.

Modern Nambé Pueblo is but a mere shadow of its former self. Less than two dozen of the original 200 or so pre-Spanish buildings have survived the years, and due to an extensive plaza reconstruction project even those have lost their traditional appearance. About 400 people reside on the 19,000-acre Nambé reservation, but most live in trailer houses or recently built HUD homes outside the old village. Intermarriage with local Hispanics has greatly diluted tribal purity and, consequently, traditional beliefs and ceremonies. And though agriculture was once an important industry at the pueblo, wage work

ARTS AND CRAFTS Nambé artisans produce a few woven belts, beaded hair clips and pendants, and a small amount of mica-flaked utility pottery. The pottery is usually colored black or red and is of poor quality.

Neither trading posts nor tribal-owned shops exist at the pueblo. The few Nambé arts and crafts produced are usually sold at various Indian fairs held throughout the summer at other pueblos.

PUBLIC CEREMONIES Nambé Feast Day, dedicated to Saint Francis, is held annually on October 4. The pueblo also hosts a Fourth of July celebration at Nambé Falls Recreation Area, 4 miles east of the village. Indian dances occur at both events.

VISITOR FACILITIES Overnight camping, picnicking, fishing, and boating (no motors) are available at Nambé Falls Recreation Area. Permits should be purchased at the governor's office. Camping costs $4 per night; picnicking, $2; fishing and boating, $3. The fishing season opens April 1 and closes September 30. A New Mexico license is required. Restrooms and drinking water are available at the campground.

Telephone (505) 455-7692

in nearby Española and Los Alamos has attracted a majority of the working adults. A few determined farmers still tend small fields of grain and food crops along the Nambé River south of the village, but these become rarer each year.

Nambé's attitude toward non-Indian visitors is one of friendliness. Tribal leaders are progressively interested in attracting more tourists to the pueblo, but since Nambé offers little in the way of arts and crafts, means are limited. To remedy that situation, several teaching programs are underway to reestablish or at least revitalize the production of traditional Nambé handicrafts. Tribal leaders have felt, and rightly so, that without more active village artisans they cannot compete with other New Mexico tribes for tourist dollars.

Nambé kiva.
Right. The new mission at Nambé.

The Pueblo of Picurís

T I W A

ORIGINAL INDIAN NAME Piwwe-tha—"Pass in the Mountains."

HOW TO GET THERE From Española, New Mexico, drive north on N.M. 68 (Taos Highway) 17 miles to the junction of N.M. 75 and turn right. Drive 24 miles and turn left onto Indian Road 120 at the Picurís Pueblo sign. The pueblo entrance is .7 mile north.

ELEVATION 7,500 feet.

HOURS 9 A.M. to 4 P.M. daily, except during closed religious ceremonies.

ADMISSION Free to enter the pueblo, but a $1 fee is charged to visit the prehistoric ruins located just north of the plaza. Permits should be purchased at the Picurís Governor's Office near the pueblo entrance.

PHOTOGRAPHY Yes. Permits cost $5 for each still camera, $10 for each movie camera, and $10 for sketching, and they may be purchased at the governor's office. Tribal officials request that visitors ask permission before taking pictures of individuals. Special permission is also required (from

San Lorenzo Mission at Picurís.

PREHISTORIC Indian tribes were living in small villages near present-day Picurís as early as 900 A.D., but archaeologists say the pueblo itself was constructed about the mid-1200s. Raiding nomads from the northern plains probably caused the earlier villagers to band together for protection.

Francisco Coronado knew that Picurís existed, but not until 1598, when Juan de Oñate took possession of New Mexico for the Spanish crown, was the pueblo actually visited by Europeans. At that time Picurís was among the largest pueblos in the province, boasting several six-story apartment-house dwellings and a population well in excess of 3,000. The first Spanish visitors considered Picurís an aggressive, warlike community—a description that in 1680 would be proven correct.

Following the initial Spanish visits remote Picurís existed quietly with little interference until about 1620, when priests began arriving. Using forced Indian labor they constructed the San Lorenzo Mission, then banned traditional Picurís religion. An iron-fisted priest, Fray Martín de Arvide, introduced La Encomienda—the system of heavy agricultural taxation that placed Picurís on the verge of starvation.

By 1680 the pueblo had had enough. Luís Tupato, governor of the pueblo, played a major role in planning and leading the Pueblo Revolt, and on August 10 Picurís lived up to its warlike reputation. During the revolt's first hours at least 20 Spaniards—many of them women and children—were killed without mercy. The San Lorenzo Mission was totally destroyed, and a few days later a large, well-armed force of Picurís warriors marched on Santa Fe to help oust Governor Otermín and his band of Spanish survivors from the province.

When Diego de Vargas reconquered New Mexico in 1692 Picurís submitted quietly to the Spaniards, but it revolted again in 1696. This time the Indians abandoned their village and joined a band of nomadic

tribal authorities) before photographing the San Lorenzo Mission.

INTERPRETIVE SERVICES Guided tours of the old Picurís Pueblo ruins are available upon request during the summer months. The guided tour as well as an excellent brochure about the pueblo are included in the $1 prehistoric-ruins charge.

The Picurís Museum and Recreation Center, located east of the governor's office, contains a small selection of prehistoric artifacts, most of them recovered in excavations of old Picurís during the 1960s. The museum is open from 9 A.M. to 6 P.M. daily, but don't be surprised to find the doors locked occasionally during working hours. Picurís time clocks do not always agree with those of the non-Indian world.

ARTS AND CRAFTS Pueblo artisans produce small amounts of bead and leather work and pottery. Traditionally Picurís pottery was black and gray, but following the Pueblo Revolt in 1680 this type of ceramics disappeared, to be replaced by bronze-colored, mica-flecked utility pottery. It is one of the few types of Indian ceramics that can be used safely for cooking. Connoisseurs of Southwestern cuisine claim that beans cooked in Picurís pots taste better than when cooked in other types of containers.

The Picurís museum sells some arts and crafts, but most pueblo artisans do business from their

Apaches in what is now southern Colorado. In the ensuing years disease and warfare with other tribes dramatically reduced the Picurís population, and in 1706, when finally its members returned to the pueblo, only 500 of the original 3,000 plus remained.

Today the population of Picurís is about 200. The pueblo, once a large, well-fortified town with hundreds of buildings, has all but disappeared. Only a few of the original mud and stone houses—most of them clustered atop a hill overlooking Pueblo Creek—have survived the years. The majority of these older homes are occupied by village elders; younger residents live in the 30 or so new HUD houses built on the village outskirts.

Unemployment rates at Picurís are high. The village is remote, and the long commute to Española or Santa Fe significantly reduces opportunities for off-reservation jobs. Most adults still scrape a living from the 15,000-acre reservation as farmers or stock growers. The tribe has developed no light industry and plays only a minor role in dictating Indian policy in New Mexico. Despite its limitations, however, Picurís is extremely friendly toward non-Indians and usually welcomes visitors enthusiastically.

A new mission, constructed about 1775 to replace the original San Lorenzo Church destroyed in the Pueblo Revolt, stands on the east side of the Picurís plaza, and with tribal permission may be visited and photographed. However, the most interesting attraction in the village is the restored portion of old Picurís. During the 1960s archaeological excavations unearthed several 700-year-old kivas and storage rooms, and these are open to visitors.

homes. Small, hand-painted signs inform visitors where to look. There are no trading posts or arts and crafts shops at the pueblo.

PUBLIC CEREMONIES   Dances and other religious celebrations are held in January, February, April, June, July, August, and December. Most are open to the public, but dates and times change from year to year. Call the pueblo before your visit for up-to-date information.

Picurís Feast Day, dedicated to pueblo patron San Lorenzo, is held annually on August 10. It is usually accompanied by a corn dance, footraces, and a pole-climbing contest.

Cameras, tape recorders, and sketch pads are strictly forbidden during all Picurís ceremonies.

VISITOR FACILITIES   Overnight camping is prohibited on the Picurís reservation, but several hundred campsites, drinking water, and restrooms are available in the Carson National Forest 10 miles east of the pueblo. Check with the ranger station in the village of Peñasco for directions and permits.

Fishing and picnicking facilities are located at Picurís Lake, a small Indian-owned recreation area adjacent to the pueblo. Permits cost $2.50 for adults and $1.50 for children under 12. A New Mexico license is required; the limit is eight trout per day.

Telephone (505) 587-2519

These old houses at Picurís have been partially reconstructed.

The Pueblo of Sandía

ORIGINAL INDIAN NAME   Nafiat— "A Dusty Place."

HOW TO GET THERE   From Albuquerque, drive north 14 miles on old U.S. 85. The pueblo entrance is on the right.

ELEVATION   5,050 feet.

HOURS   8 A.M. until sundown, except during closed religious ceremonies.

ADMISSION   Free. Visitors should obtain permission to walk in the pueblo from the Sandía Governor's Office.

PHOTOGRAPHY   No. Cameras, tape recorders, and sketch pads are absolutely forbidden.

INTERPRETIVE SERVICES   None; no brochures available.

ARTS AND CRAFTS   Sandía produces very few arts or crafts. Pueblo artisans make a small amount of rough, dark pottery and a few traditional paintings, and they do some basket weaving and leather work. There are no trading posts or stores in the village; Sandía arts and

San Antonio Mission at Sandía.

S ANDÍA Pueblo was constructed around 1300 A.D., probably by migrating clans of Anasazi from what is now Arizona. Hernándo de Alvarado, captain under the command of Francisco Coronado, was the first European to visit the village, in 1540. He gave Sandía its present name after mistaking a local variety of squash for *sandía*, which is Spanish for watermelon.

This pueblo was one of the original 12 towns of Tiguex in which Coronado spent the winter of 1540–1541, but whether it was burned by the conquistador (see *Introduction*) is unknown. After Coronado returned to Mexico Sandía was unmolested until the arrival of Juan de Oñate in 1598. Sixteen years later the Mission of San Francisco was constructed in the village, and Christianization of the residents began. When in 1680 the Pueblo Revolt came to pass Sandía took an active role. Pueblo warriors killed several resident Spaniards and burned the mission to the ground.

A year after the Revolt, when former New Mexico governor Otermín attempted a reconquest, Sandía was sacked and burned. Having no village for shelter and fearing further Spanish reprisals, the Indians fled westward to the Hopi region and there constructed the village of Payupki on Second Mesa. The ruins of this now-abandoned Tiwa pueblo may still be seen.

In 1742, thanks to the urging of a Spanish priest, the Sandía people were persuaded to return to New Mexico and rebuild their original village. Another mission, this one dedicated to Saint Anthony, was constructed on the site of the ruined San Francisco Church. It stood until 1880, when from misuse it collapsed. The mission now standing at Sandía was built shortly before the turn of the century.

Frankly, except on Feast Day there is little for visitors to do or see at Sandía. About 250 people reside on the 22,000-acre reservation,

crafts are sold exclusively through the Pueblo Indian Cultural Center in Albuquerque.

PUBLIC CEREMONIES Jealously guarding its traditional religious ceremonies, Sandía opens few of its rites to the public. Feast Day, held annually on June 13 and dedicated to patron Saint Anthony, is perhaps the only celebration of interest to visitors.

VISITOR FACILITIES None. Overnight camping and motel accommodations are available in Bernalillo, 4 miles north of the pueblo on U.S. 85.

Telephone (505) 867-2876

but most adults hold off-reservation jobs in nearby Albuquerque. Most of the structures in the main village were built in the 1700s, but decades of paint and stucco have removed any architectural beauty the old buildings might once have displayed.

Farming has all but disappeared at Sandía. However, recently tribal officials have initiated an agricultural project they hope will not only retrieve interest in farming but also turn into a money-making venture. A 20-acre you-pick-it operation, whereby visitors will be able to gather corn, squash, melons, and chiles directly from the fields, is expected to be in full swing by the summer of 1984.

Sandía circa 1910.
Right. Sandía pottery.

The Pueblo of San Felipe

ORIGINAL INDIAN NAME   Katish-tya — meaning unknown.

HOW TO GET THERE   From Albuquerque, drive north on Interstate 25 about 22 miles. Turn left off the freeway at the San Felipe Pueblo sign. The pueblo entrance is about 3 miles farther.

ELEVATION   5,200 feet.

HOURS   8 A.M. to 6 P.M. daily, except during closed religious celebrations.

ADMISSION   Free, but visitors should obtain permission to walk in the village from the tribal administrator's office. Non-Indians are not permitted to visit the San Felipe Mission.

THE original Katishtya village was located a few miles west of present-day San Felipe and was first visited by Coronado in 1540. Little else is known of the pueblo except that San Felipe ancestors were probably homeless Anasazi from the Four Corners region of New Mexico, Colorado, Utah, and Arizona.

In 1598 Katishtya fell under the domination of a Spanish priest named Fray Juan de Rozas, and the first mission was built there in 1605. A few years later the pueblo rebelled, but the uprising was crushed by Spanish cavalry. When the Pueblo Revolt took place in 1680 Katishtya warriors were quick to join, killing several resident priests. Not long after the Indians burned the church, abandoned the village, and retreated to the mountains with neighbors from nearby Cóchiti and Santo Domingo pueblos.

Twelve years later Diego de Vargas discovered the Katishtya residents living in a new village atop Tamita Mesa (a mile west of the present village site). Fearing the superior weapons of the Spaniards, the Indians took an oath of obedience and a year later assisted de Vargas in overcoming another revolt staged by Santo Domingo and Cóchiti. About 1700 the Tamita Mesa village was abandoned and the present pueblo of San Felipe was founded. A new mission was constructed there in 1706.

San Felipe pottery.

PHOTOGRAPHY No. Cameras, tape recorders, and sketch pads are strictly forbidden. They will be confiscated if found in the pueblo by tribal officials.

INTERPRETIVE SERVICES None; no brochures available.

ARTS AND CRAFTS Very little pottery has been made in San Felipe since about 1700—the few bowls that artisans do produce are usually dark, rough, and nontraditional. There is one Indian-owned shop in the village—the Calabaza Indian House Shop, located near the pueblo entrance. A small collection of San Felipe pottery, turquoise jewelry, and leather work is displayed here.

PUBLIC CEREMONIES Dances are held at San Felipe in January, February, April, May, June, and August, but dates and times vary from year to year. Call the pueblo before your visit for up-to-date information.

San Felipe Feast Day is May 1. It is accompanied by the green corn dance, one of the most spectacular ceremonies held by pueblo Indians. All day long, several hundred men and women attired in traditional costumes snake through the San Felipe plaza, singing and chanting to Keresan spirits who control the rainfall and corn growth.

VISITOR FACILITIES None. Motel accommodations are available in Albuquerque, Bernalillo, and Santa Fe.

Telephone (505) 867-3381

San Felipe Pueblo today is one of the most conservative of all New Mexican pueblos. The tribal administration, extremely traditional in its views, is only mildly interested in tourism, non-Indians, or the outside world in general. Unfortunately, because tribal regulations have become so strict, many young San Felipans have left the pueblo permanently to take off-reservation jobs in Albuquerque and Santa Fe.

The physical arrangement of the pueblo has changed very little in the past 300 years. The main part of San Felipe surrounds a large central plaza in an "enclosed fortress" type of architecture common in pre-Spanish times. Two large kivas near the village center are still used for the many secret ceremonies that take place in San Felipe each year. Thirty-five modern HUD homes have been constructed during the last decade, but by order of the conservative tribal council all are well outside the boundaries of the old village.

The San Felipe reservation encompasses 49,000 acres. Many of the pueblo's 2,500 residents are farmers, tending small irrigated plots of alfalfa and grain crops in the bottomland of the nearby Río Grande. Since there is little to do or see in the village and residents are sometimes hostile toward outsiders, visits to San Felipe are not recommended except during Feast Day.

Deer dancer doll from San Felipe Pueblo.

The old church at San Felipe
circa 1899.

The Pueblo of San Ildefonso

ORIGINAL INDIAN NAME   Powohgeonwige — "Where the Water Cuts
Down Through."

HOW TO GET THERE   From Santa Fe,
drive 15 miles north on U.S. 84–
285 to the junction of N.M. 4 (Los
Alamos Highway). Turn left. The
pueblo entrance is about 6 miles
beyond on the right.

ELEVATION   5,500 feet.

HOURS   8 A.M. to 5 P.M. daily.

ADMISSION   Free; permission not
required. Visitors are requested not
to go near the kiva at the south end
of San Ildefonso plaza.

PHOTOGRAPHY   Yes. Photo permits
cost $2 for each still camera, $5 for
each movie camera, and $3 for
sketch pads; they may be purchased at the governor's office.
Tribal officials ask only that you
obtain individual permissions
before taking pictures of people.

ELDERS of San Ildefonso say their ancestors came originally from the great Anasazi community of Mesa Verde, stopping first to construct and inhabit the villages of Tyuonyi and Tsankawi in present-day Bandelier National Monument. Probably because of harsh drought these two towns were abandoned around 1300 A.D., and archaeologists think the inhabitants moved into the Río Grande Valley to build the village of Perage ("Place of the Kangaroo Rat"), a mile west of present-day San Ildefonso.

It was Perage that Francisco Leyva de Bonilla, the first European to visit the San Ildefonso Indians, discovered in 1593. A few years later, probably because of worn-out, overworked farmland, the Indians aban- doned Perage and moved across the Río Grande to the present site of San Ildefonso. About 1617 a large mission was constructed by Spanish priests in the village.

During the next half century, heavy agricultural taxation and prohibition of traditional Indian religion caused lean times and hard feelings at San Ildefonso, and during the Pueblo Revolt in 1680 village warriors happily helped put Santa Fe to the torch. Surprisingly, how- ever, the great mission at the pueblo went untouched during the vio- lence and was still standing when Diego de Vargas began the recon- quest of New Mexico 12 years later. Upon de Vargas's arrival San

Part of the old pueblo at San Ildefonso.

INTERPRETIVE SERVICES   No guided tours available, but a free brochure that includes a history of the pueblo and a list of all San Ildefonso artists is available for the asking at the governor's office. A small museum located in the Tribal Administration Building displays a collection of pueblo artifacts as well as examples of contemporary arts and crafts. Its summer hours are 8 A.M. to 4:30 P.M.; winter hours, 8 A.M. to noon.

ARTS AND CRAFTS   San Ildefonso is home to nearly 40 full-time pottery makers and painters, many of whom are famous throughout the world. The best known of all was potter María Martínez. In 1919,

Ildefonso quickly capitulated, but in 1694 the pueblo broke its promise of peace and, with other Tewa tribes from Santa Clara and Tesuque, took refuge atop Black Mesa, a steep-sided basalt mountain north of the village. With two cannon and 100 men, de Vargas placed the fortress-peak under siege in an attempt to starve the rebellious tribes into submission. Two weeks later, however, the Spaniards retreated, themselves low on food and ammunition. Atop Black Mesa 40 Tewa warriors lay dead and several score had been wounded, but the Tewa had won the field.

Of their own accord, San Ildefonso residents returned to their pueblo and signed another declaration of peace. But again, two years later, the pueblo revolted against Spanish domination, this time burning the mission to the ground before retreating to Black Mesa. And again, de Vargas placed the mountain under siege. Unable to withstand repeated attacks from Spanish cavalry, the Indians finally surrendered and were returned under guard to the pueblo. There, for the next three centuries, they remained.

María and her husband developed a process for making polished black pottery with a matte-black design. So new and unusual was the style that it quickly caught the eye of collectors, and within a few years María had gained worldwide recognition. By the time of her death, in 1980, a signed María bowl or vase was virtually priceless.

Several shops in which visitors may examine or purchase San Ildefonso handicrafts are located in the pueblo. The Studio of Indian Arts, located just south of the mission, displays all types of arts and crafts, including a polychrome ware with turquoise inlay made by María's son, Popovi Da. The Aguilar Shop, located at the south end of the plaza, offers mostly paintings. In addition, there are numerous shops in private homes throughout the pueblo. Look for "Pottery for Sale" or "Paintings for Sale" signs tacked to trees or doorways.

Left. Black on black and polychrome pottery from San Ildefonso.
Right. San Ildefonso kiva.

As a whole, the present-day community of San Ildefonso is progressive but still strongly bonded to its ancient heritage. On one hand, the value of the dollar is well known by pueblo residents; on the other, tribal religion and practice of ancient traditions is a daily affair, tenacious even after nearly 300 years of white man's influence. More and more young people are attending college, but instead of seeking permanent jobs elsewhere many are returning to the pueblo to offer their talents and knowledge to the tribe.

PUBLIC CEREMONIES   Indian dances are held at San Ildefonso during January, June, July, September, and December. Dates usually vary from year to year. For up-to-date information, call the pueblo well in advance of your visit.

San Ildefonso Feast Day is held annually on January 23, and it is accompanied by dancing. Usually, but not always, cameras are permitted at the ceremonies. A Feast Day permit costs $5 and may be obtained at the governor's office.

VISITOR FACILITIES   No overnight camping. Motel accommodations are available in nearby Los Alamos, Española, or Santa Fe.

A small trout pond a mile southwest of the pueblo is open during the summer months. Check at the governor's office for regulations and permit costs.

Telephone (505) 786-5302

San Ildefonso consists of 216 structures haphazardly scattered around a large, manicured plaza. Many of the original buildings have undergone reconstruction, yet careful planning during the various face-lifts has retained most of the traditional Tewa architecture. In 1957 an old church, built on the site of the original but considered ugly by most of the tribe, was demolished. Raised in its place was a perfect replica of the 17th-century mission burned during the third San Ildefonso revolt. And even official buildings must conform to the tribe's strict construction code; when the new, ultramodern Tribal Administration Building was erected recently, it was built in typical pueblo style.

At one time farming was an important enterprise on the 30,000-acre San Ildefonso reservation, but because of water shortages agricultural pursuits have declined substantially in the last decade. Today, most of the pueblo's 430 permanent residents not involved with arts and crafts production work in Los Alamos or Santa Fe.

Right. The mission at San Ildefonso.

The Pueblo of San Juan

ORIGINAL INDIAN NAME   O'ke or Ohke—"Hard Grinding Stone."

HOW TO GET THERE   From Española, New Mexico, drive a mile north on N.M. 68 (Taos Highway) and turn left onto U.S. 285 at the "San Juan Pueblo" sign. The pueblo entrance is .6 mile farther.

ELEVATION   5,500 feet.

HOURS   8 A.M. to 5 P.M., Monday through Saturday. Portions of the pueblo may be closed to the public during religious ceremonies.

ADMISSION   Free. However, permission and an escort are required to enter the old section of San Juan. You should inquire at the governor's office.

PHOTOGRAPHY   Yes. Photo permits cost $5 for each camera and should be purchased at the San Juan Police Department or Governor's Office. No restrictions apply.

Left. Basket dancers at San Juan Pueblo.
Right. San Juan Pueblo boy in front of traditional dwelling.

A s is the case with most Río Grande pueblos, archaeologists think the, ancestry of San Juan originated with migrating clans of Anasazi, driven by drought from their traditional homes in what is now the Four Corners region.

Indian legends claim the present-day pueblo is the third to be inhabited by the people of San Juan. The first two were a mile north and were destroyed by floods in pre-Spanish times. Both were named O'ke.

In 1540, Francisco Coronado knew of O'ke's existence but did not visit the pueblo. The first European actually to make contact with O'ke was treasure-chaser Castaño de Sosa, in 1591. "The very sight of us," wrote Castaño after his short visit, "frightened the inhabitants,

INTERPRETIVE SERVICES   A selection of pueblo artifacts and exhibits is on display at the Eight Northern Pueblos Council Headquarters Building, at the north end of the village. Admission is free. No brochures are available.

ARTS AND CRAFTS   Recently San Juan has experienced an arts and crafts revival, and today it is one of the leading tourist suppliers for Indian-made handicrafts. Local artisans produce finely incised pottery, coral and turquoise jewelry, embroidery, leather and bead work, weavings, and baskets. Most San Juan arts and crafts are priced reasonably and are of excellent quality.

Two large Indian-owned-and-operated crafts stores are open daily at the pueblo. O'ke Oweenge Crafts Cooperative, located adjacent to Our Lady of Lourdes shrine, offers an excellent selection of all types of San Juan handicrafts, most of it produced by graduates of the cooperative's arts and crafts training program. The Artisans' Guild, a block south of the San Juan Mission, sells both traditional and contemporary creations from all eight northern pueblos.

especially the women, who wept a great deal."

In July 1598, Governor Capt. Gen. Juan de Oñate—following orders from Spain to colonize and pacify New Mexico—proclaimed O'ke the capital of the province. Oñate ordered the Indians to leave the pueblo, then he and his men and 7,000 head of livestock moved in. The Spaniards changed the pueblo's name to San Juan de los Caballeros ("Saint John of the Gentlemen") and promptly confiscated all Indian possessions in the village. The Indians, ejected into the countryside, were forced to rely on assistance from neighboring villages merely to survive.

A month later Oñate moved to the nearby pueblo of Yugeuingge (now abandoned), ousted the inhabitants, and renamed the town San Gabriel. Here he built the San Gabriel Mission, the first church to be constructed in what is now the United States. The residents of O'ke were allowed to return to their newly renamed and badly looted village.

For the next three-quarters of a century the Indians of San Juan were harassed and mistreated by the Spaniards, especially by the priests. Then, in 1675, 47 religious leaders from several different pueblos were arrested on charges of witchcraft. Some were hanged; the others, publicly flogged. One of the latter was Po Pay (also spelled *Pope*), a San Juan medicine man who from the moment of his release began plotting the overthrow and expulsion of the Spanish.

Po Pay's grand design was realized five years later when, in 1680, the Pueblo Revolt occurred and the Spaniards were ejected. Twelve years later, of course, they were back, and in 1692 San Juan signed an oath of obedience to the Spanish. Shortly thereafter the first mission, dedicated to Saint John, was constructed at the pueblo. The church stood until 1913, when the crumbling structure was replaced by the New England–type building seen today.

Modern San Juan is perhaps the most progressive of all Southwestern pueblos. Headquarters of the Eight Northern Pueblos Council (an all-Indian organization established in 1965 to better conditions in the pueblos), San Juan plays an important role in dictating statewide Indian policy. It has also been a leader in the rebirth of pueblo arts and crafts production.

PUBLIC CEREMONIES Dances and religious ceremonies are held in January, February, April, June, July, and December. Call the pueblo before your visit for exact times and dates.

San Juan Feast Day is held annually on June 24 and is usually accompanied by the Comanche dance.

VISITOR FACILITIES None. Overnight camping facilities and motel accommodations are available in Española.

Telephone (505) 852-4400

New construction is the norm at the pueblo. The police force, Eight Northern Pueblos Council headquarters, Arts and Crafts Co-op, and the Artisan's Guild all are housed in new, ultramodern buildings, and more than 250 HUD homes are scattered throughout the village. The tribe administers two industrial parks south of the pueblo, owns and operates an adobe (mud brick) plant, and leases tribal land to a local lumber company. However, tradition has not been forgotten. About 100 original, 700-year-old homes in the pueblo are still in existence, and most are being renovated. Tribal religion is still healthy and, in many homes at least, dictates almost every facet of daily life.

The San Juan reservation encompasses 12,000 acres, and the pueblo population is about 1,400. Farming and stock raising are important sources of revenue to many residents, but better paying off-reservation jobs are becoming more common among working adults.

San Juan tribal elder.

The Pueblo of Santa Clara

TEWA

ORIGINAL INDIAN NAME   K'hapoo—
"Where the Wild Roses Grow Near
the Water."

HOW TO GET THERE   From Española,
New Mexico, drive 1.3 miles north
on N.M. 5 (on the west side of the
Rio Grande). The well-marked
pueblo entrance is on the left.

ELEVATION   5,600 feet.

HOURS   8 A.M. to 5 P.M. The tribal
administration office is closed on
Sundays.

ADMISSION   Free. Permission is
not required to walk through the
pueblo or to visit the mission.

PHOTOGRAPHY   Yes; permits are
not required. Tribal officials ask
that you obtain permission from
individuals before taking their
pictures. Photography is allowed
during pueblo dances but only
with permission from individual
performers.

INTERPRETIVE SERVICES   A mimeo-
graphed brochure about Santa
Clara is available at the governor's
office.

*Ceremonial dancers from Santa
Clara Pueblo at Puye Cliffs.*

THE village of K'hapoo was probably constructed in the early 14th century by wandering clans of Anasazi from the present-day Four Corners region. The village was later joined by the inhabitants of Puye Cliffs, who abandoned their mesa-top dwellings around 1500 because of severe drought. In 1540 the pueblo was visited by Capt. Hernándo de Alvarado, but little is known of the occasion or of pueblo activities between then and the completion in 1629 of the first Santa Clara Mission.

During the Pueblo Revolt in 1680, a small detachment of Spanish soldiers stationed at Santa Clara were killed and the mission was burned to the ground. Twelve years later, when Diego de Vargas returned to New Mexico, pueblo leaders signed an oath of obedience, but two years after that the Santa Clarans revolted again and joined with other Tewa tribes atop nearby Black Mesa. (See *The Pueblo of San Ildefonso.*) When in 1696 they were finally forced by Spanish troops to surrender, many Santa Clarans fled west to the Hopi and Zuni pueblos and remained there until 1702, when they were coaxed back to their original village by Spanish priests. A new mission was erected early in the 1700s but collapsed in a storm in 1910. The present mission was constructed about 1918.

Today, nearly 2,000 people reside on the 46,000-acre Santa Clara reservation. Traditional religious activities still play an important role in pueblo life, but young, well-educated tribal leaders are slowly nudging the village toward a more progressive attitude. Modern housing and large new community structures are the norm now. Many of the original pueblo dwellings, some dating back 700 years, have been demolished to make way for the new construction.

A good number of farmers still tend fields in the rich bottomland along the Río Grande, or graze cattle and sheep in the nearby

ARTS AND CRAFTS   Most Santa Clara artisans are potters, producing large amounts of polychrome and black-on-black ware (the latter style borrowed from San Ildefonso about 1927). Both are of excellent quality and make good investments. Surprisingly, however, the two best-known Santa Clara artists are painters. Pablita Velarde and her daughter Helen Hardin have both gained worldwide recognition with Southwestern Indian scenes.

The Singing Man, an Indian-owned shop situated on N.M. 5 near the pueblo entrance, offers a wide selection of locally produced arts and crafts. Most pueblo artisans also sell from their homes. Look for signs or ask at the governor's office.

The works of Pablita Velarde and Helen Hardin can be seen at Enchanted Mesa Indian Arts in Albuquerque.

PUBLIC CEREMONIES   Dances and other ceremonies are held in Santa Clara in January, February, March, April, June, August, and December. Exact dates and times vary from year to year, so call the pueblo before your visit.

Santa Clara Feast Day is held annually on August 12 and is usually accompanied by the corn dance. Recording devices and sketch pads are forbidden at all pueblo religious ceremonies.

mountains, but Santa Clara, like San Ildefonso, has contributed a large percentage of its working adults to the government facility at Los Alamos. Usage fees from Santa Clara Canyon Recreation Area and large tracts of reservation land leased to the city of Española bring in a substantial annual income. Consequently, unemployment rates are low at the pueblo, and the Santa Clara tribe as a whole has become relatively wealthy.

One of the most successful and well known Santa Clara Indians was Dr. Edward Dozier. Author of more than 50 articles and books on North American Indians, Dr. Dozier was the first Santa Clara resident to receive a doctoral degree from an American university. He died in 1971 and is buried at the pueblo.

Left and right. Eagle dancers and drummers at Santa Clara.

VISITOR FACILITIES   Overnight camping, picnicking, and trout fishing are available at the Santa Clara Canyon Recreation Area, located 9 miles southwest of the pueblo on N.M. 5. Camping permits are $5; picnicking is $3; and fishing, $3. All permits can be purchased at the Santa Clara ranger station at the mouth of the canyon. The recreation area is open from April 1 to October 31. Hours for picnicking and fishing are 6 A.M. to 9 P.M.

Puye Cliffs, an abandoned, 2,000-room Anasazi village built between 1400 and 1450 A.D., sits just off N.M. 5 in the lower portion of Santa Clara Canyon. It's open to the public from April through October.

Until recently Santa Clara Pueblo held an annual arts and crafts fair at Puye, but the ceremony was permanently cancelled in 1981 after lightning struck and killed several fairgoers. At least according to legend, it was not the first time tragedy had struck at Puye. During archaeological excavations in the 1930s, several Indian workers heard ghostly voices saying "Don't take me from this ground." Some of the workers, so goes the story, continued digging and suddenly died.

Telephone (505) 753-7326

The Pueblo of Santo Domingo

K E R E S A N

ORIGINAL INDIAN NAME   Guipui —
meaning unknown.

HOW TO GET THERE   From Albuquerque, drive 30 miles north on
Interstate 25 to the junction of
N.M. 22 and turn left. Drive 4
miles to the junction of Indian 84.
Turn right; the pueblo entrance is
about 2 miles beyond.

ELEVATION   5,200 feet.

HOURS   9 A.M. to 5 P.M. daily,
except during closed religious
ceremonies.

ADMISSION   Free; however, permission is required from the governor's office if you plan to visit
the old village on foot.

PHOTOGRAPHY   No. Cameras, tape
recorders, and sketch pads will be
confiscated immediately if they are
discovered by tribal officials.

INTERPRETIVE SERVICES   None; no
brochures available.

*Santo Domingo woman
making fry bread.*

THE Santo Domingo we see today is a relatively new pueblo, occupied only since the late 1800s. It is the fourth or fifth village of Guipui, however; the others were destroyed by flood waters of the Río Grande.

Santo Domingo was given its Spanish name in 1591 by Castaño de Sosa, the first European to visit the pueblo. In 1598 Capt. Gen. Juan de Oñate, New Mexico's first governor, met with tribal leaders from about 30 pueblos at Santo Domingo. Oñate demanded and received allegiance from the Indians, not only to God and the Spanish king but to himself as well. Pueblo leaders were told they would suffer "cruel and everlasting torment" if they were not baptized immediately. To assist in this soul-saving crusade, Oñate ordered a monastery to be constructed at Santo Domingo. Seven years after its completion, both monastery and pueblo were destroyed by a massive flood.

In 1607 another village was established nearby, and in it the first Santo Domingo mission constructed. During the next seven decades heavy Spanish taxation often nudged the Indians to the edge of starvation, and in 1680 the village quickly joined the Pueblo Revolt. Santo Domingo warriors killed all three resident Spanish priests and sent a large force to attack Santa Fe. Afterward, in anticipation of Spanish reprisals, the pueblo was abandoned, but it was reoccupied when no soldiers appeared.

When Diego de Vargas reconquered New Mexico 12 years later, tribal leaders from the pueblo signed an oath of obedience, then promptly retreated to a mountain stronghold with Indians from the Jemez region. In 1694 de Vargas and his soldiers, assisted by a company of Indians friendly to them, stormed the fortified camp, killing 90 warriors in the process and capturing 300 women and children. Meanwhile, another group of Santo Domingos joined with refugees from

ARTS AND CRAFTS Santo Domingo artisans produce fine strings of heishie—disc-shaped beads of bone, shell, and turquoise—as well as silver and turquoise jewelry. There are several potters in the pueblo, but most make only "tourist pots"—small, garishly painted bowls and vases that are of substandard quality. The best Santo Domingo ceramics are produced by a 30-year-old potter named Robert Tenorio, whose traditional black-and-cream-on-red ware has won numerous regional and national awards.

Most Santo Domingo artists are itinerant folk, selling their handicrafts at art shows, flea markets, and from temporary street shops throughout the Southwest. A favored location is beneath the South Portal at the Palace of the Governors in nearby Santa Fe. Robert Tenorio's pottery can be seen at the Wheelwright Museum, located in the museum complex in Santa Fe.

Collectors of Indian jewelry offer this piece of advice when buying Santo Domingo handicrafts: "Be wary." Quite often, items sold as bone and shell are nothing more than plastic, and necklaces and bracelets advertised as turquoise are, in reality, only turquoise dust mixed with epoxy. You should also know that most Santo Domingo artisans are usually willing to bargain; don't settle for the price marked on the item you wish to buy.

neighboring Cóchiti Pueblo and fled to the village of Cieneguilla. This group too was attacked and defeated by the Spaniards. By 1696 most of the Santo Domingos had returned to their pueblo, though a few survivors escaped west toward Ácoma, there to found the Pueblo of Laguna in 1699. However, fate had not yet finished its work at Santo Domingo. About 1700 both pueblo and mission were destroyed by flood. Both were rebuilt, only to be again washed away in 1885. They were rebuilt once more shortly thereafter, and it is this village that stands today.

Present-day Santo Domingo is frankly an unfriendly pueblo, and except during the annual Feast Day on August 4, a visit cannot be recommended. Tribal leaders neither promote nor seek tourism, and the official attitude toward non-Indian visitors, though many pueblo residents (especially the local artisans) don't necessarily agree with it, is extremely conservative and sometimes downright hostile. On Feast Day, tourists are tolerated only as long as they strictly adhere to tribal policies.

The Santo Domingo reservation consists of 69,000 acres. Most pueblo adults are either farmers or are involved in the arts and crafts industry; very few hold off-reservation jobs. Village life is highly traditional, and tribal religion plays an important role in both private and official activities. Most Santo Domingo Indians do not hesitate to say that the mission exists only for the priests, and the kivas belong to the people.

Dances and other religious ceremonies open to the public are held in January, June, and December. Dates vary, however; call the pueblo before your visit for up-to-date information.

Santo Domingo Feast Day occurs on August 4. The accompanying corn dance is the largest of all pueblo dances. More than 500 Indians take part.

The pueblo absolutely prohibits cameras, tape recorders, and sketch pads on tribal lands at any time, but especially during religious ceremonies. Crowd monitors will forcibly (if necessary) confiscate such items on the spot, and quite often the offender will receive a stiff fine.

VISITOR FACILITIES   None.

Telephone (505) 465-2214

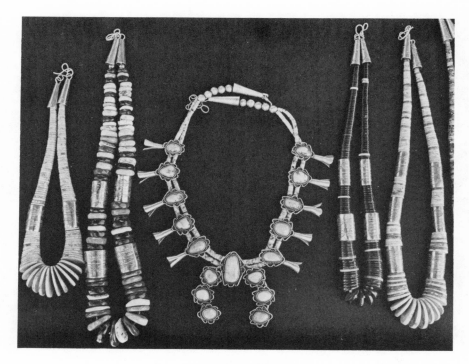

Traditional Santo Domingo crafts.

The Pueblo of Taos

T I W A

ORIGINAL INDIAN NAME Tua-tah— "Our Village."

HOW TO GET THERE Taos Pueblo is 2 miles north of the city of Taos; the pueblo entrance road turns off N.M. 68 on the north side of town. It is well marked.

ELEVATION 7,900 feet.

HOURS Summer, 8 A.M. to 6 P.M.; winter, 9 A.M. to 5 P.M.

ADMISSION $3 per person. Permits must be purchased at the registration office near the pueblo entrance. Tribal officials request that visitors stay clear of the well-marked restricted zones.

PHOTOGRAPHY Yes. Permits cost $5 per camera and must be purchased at the registration office. Visitors may take pictures anywhere within village boundaries except inside the San Geronimo Mission. Ask permission before photographing individual Indians.

INTERPRETIVE SERVICES None. Brochures unavailable.

Left. Taos Pueblo elder.
Right. Traditional dwellings at Taos.

THE region around Taos was occupied as early as 900 A.D. By 1300, the Indians were living in several small villages within a mile of the present-day pueblo site. Indian legends, passed from generation to generation by word of mouth, say Taos ancestors once lived on the edge of a large lake known as Mojua-lua, located somewhere in the mountains to the east.

In 1540 Capt. Hernándo de Alvarado, the most wide ranging of all Coronado's soldiers, visited Tua-tah and, at least according to old Spanish records, was pleasantly received by its inhabitants. The village Alvarado saw was not the same one that stands today, but in size, shape, and location was similar. Alvarado named the town Braba and estimated the total population at 15,000 (likely a gross exaggeration). Braba was, the Spaniard said, a large trading center doing a healthy business with Comanche and Apache Indians in food, skins, textiles, and pottery.

ARTS AND CRAFTS Taos artisans produce woven textiles, drums, leather and bead work, and a small amount of undecorated utility pottery with a micaceous finish. Several shops exist in the pueblo where visitors can purchase local arts and crafts. Romero's Curio Shop is located in the center of the North Pueblo, facing the plaza. The owner, Mrs. Romero, is one of the pueblo's best potters. Lujan's Trading Post is situated across from the San Geronimo Mission adjacent to the registration office; it offers a wide selection of rings, bracelets, pottery, and bead work. The Morningtalk Shop and Red Shirt Drum Shop are located west of the pueblo on the entrance road.

The next European to see Tua-tah, or Braba, was Juan de Oñate in 1598. Oñate changed the name to Taos and ordered a mission to be constructed. Three decades later, resident priests reported that 2,500 Indians had been converted to Christianity and baptized. However, Spanish rule was unacceptable to the Indians, and in 1639 the people of Taos abandoned village and church and moved east into what is now Kansas. They were tracked down and returned by Spanish soldiers two years later.

By 1680 Taos was a hotbed of discontent. Po Pay, the San Juan medicine man who had sworn to remove the Spanish from the Southwest, was living underground in the village, and most of the plans for the Pueblo Revolt had been made and preparations put in operation. (See *The Pueblo of San Juan.*) On August 10, when the uprising finally occurred, Taos warriors killed two priests and several Spanish settlers who lived in the vicinity, burned the mission, then marched on Santa Fe.

When Diego de Vargas returned to New Mexico in 1692, Taos

Elder, North Pueblo, Taos.

PUBLIC CEREMONIES Dances, foot-races, and other religiously oriented ceremonies are held at Taos in January, May, June, July, August, September, and December. Dates vary from year to year, so call the pueblo before your visit.

The San Geronimo Feast Day occurs annually on September 30 and is accompanied by an arts and crafts fair, footraces, a pole-climbing contest, and various dances. A sundown dance is held on the evening preceding Feast Day.

Cameras, tape recorders, and sketch pads are strictly prohibited during any religious ceremony.

Throughout Taos's early history it was a trading center for both Apache and Comanche tribes. Consequently dance costumes and the Taos dances themselves closely resemble those of the Plains Indians. Experts say Taos's dancers are among the most skilled in all the pueblos.

was one of the first pueblos against which he marched. When the Spaniards reached the village, however, it was empty; the Indians had received advance warning and had fled to the nearby mountains. Nine months later de Vargas tried again, but again the Indians had fled. Frustrated, the Spaniard burned the village to the ground. A short time later, Taos leaders signed an oath of obedience and, as a shaky peace was instigated, began rebuilding the pueblo. After three years, however, Taos revolted again, killing 26 Spaniards in the process and then fleeing the remains of their village. Again de Vargas marched, this time cornering the Indians in their mountain stronghold and forcing a surrender. Peace came, finally, and by 1700 a new pueblo and mission were under construction.

During the next 150 years guardianship of New Mexico was passed from Spain to Mexico and finally to the United States. However, many Mexicans refused to recognize American authority. When the government changed some of them incited the Taos Indians to revolt, and in 1847 warriors murdered New Mexico governor Charles Bent and several other Americans. Shortly thereafter 320 American troops arrived to restore order, and 700 Indians barricaded themselves in the San Geronimo mission and refused to surrender. With little

VISITOR FACILITIES   None. Motel accommodations can be found in the city of Taos; overnight camping, picnicking, and fishing facilities are available in Rio Grande Gorge State Park, 16 miles southwest of the pueblo just off N.M. 68.

Telephone (505) 758-8628

choice, the American commander used artillery to literally blow the church walls apart. One hundred fifty Indians died in the assault, and following the execution of 7 others for their part in the uprising peace was again restored.

Present-day Taos, snuggled beneath the sweeping slopes of 13,160-foot-high Wheeler Peak, is one of the most beautiful and traditional of all New Mexico pueblos. Divided by the Taos River into the North and South pueblos, it is a multistoried apartment-house affair, closely resembling what prehistoric pueblos must have looked like. By tribal consent electricity and telephones are prohibited in the village, and many of the upper-story rooms are still reached only by ladder. A large proportion of the older residents speak nothing but their native Tiwa.

Visitors to Taos will find a variety of sights and activities, especially during the summer months. Besides the permanent shops around the plaza, many concessions for bread, sweets, and arts and crafts are based in homes. Taos Indians are usually hospitable to tourists and occasionally invite outsiders into their homes.

The ruins of the old San Geronimo Mission lie northwest of the registration office and are open to visitors. The interior of the church is now a cemetery for the pueblo's Christian converts, and many of the gravestones are more than a century old. The location of the original mission built in the early 1600s is unknown. The new church, small and without much beauty, was constructed in the 1960s.

Earlier in this century a site sacred to the Taos Indians known as Blue Lake, situated in the mountains east of the pueblo, was included in the Carson National Forest; thereafter it was overrun by campers. The Indians objected strenuously, and, after a 50-year court battle, in 1971 the land was returned to the tribe.

The Taos reservation encompasses 9,500 acres with a tribal population of about 1,800. Most working adults are farmers or stock raisers and pay little attention to the off-reservation world. Tribal religion is extremely strong in the pueblo, and the word of the Tribal Council is law.

Breadoven in Taos.

The Pueblo of Tesuque

T E W A

ORIGINAL INDIAN NAME Taytsoon-gay—"Cottonwood Tree Place."

HOW TO GET THERE From Santa Fe, drive north on U.S. 84–285 about 10 miles. The pueblo entrance road is on the left and is well marked.

ELEVATION 5,700 feet.

HOURS 9 A.M. to 5 P.M. daily except during closed religious holidays. The tribal administration office is not open on weekends.

ADMISSION Free. Permission is not required to walk through the pueblo.

PHOTOGRAPHY Yes, in the plaza area only. Permit costs vary from year to year but are usually about $5 per camera. Permits should be purchased at the tribal administration office.

INTERPRETIVE SERVICES None. No brochures available.

ARTS AND CRAFTS During the 1960s and 1970s, arts and crafts production at Tesuque Pueblo

Tesuque children and their teacher.

THE present site of Tesuque Pueblo has been occupied since about 1700. Taytsoonghay, the village of precolonial times, was situated about 3 miles east and was founded about 1300. Like most other Tewas, the people of Tesuque believe their ancestors originated far to the north in the underworld beneath a lake known as Sandy Place. They were allowed to populate the Southwest only after many trials by fire with spiritual inhabitants of the lake.

Hernándo de Alvarado, Coronado's wide-ranging scout, was probably the first European to visit Taytsoonghay, in 1540. Gaspar Castaño de Sosa camped there in 1591 and later wrote that the village was small—no more than 200 inhabitants. Between Castaño's visit and 1680, however, almost nothing is known of Taytsoonghay's history. A mission was probably constructed there during the early 1600s, but of this church no record exists. Then on August 9, 1680, village warriors struck the first blow of the Pueblo Revolt by killing a civil servant named Cristóbal de Herrera. The following morning, Fray Juan Pio—the first priest to be dispatched in the Revolt—was murdered when he arrived at the pueblo to say mass.

After the uprising the people of Taytsoonghay abandoned their village, and for the next 14 years they lived in temporary camps in the mountainous terrain to the west. Joining inhabitants of Santa Clara and San Ildefonso pueblos, they fought Diego de Vargas at Black Mesa in 1694 and 1696, then finally returned to the Tesuque Valley (the name Taytsoonghay had by this time become corrupted to Tesuque) about 1700 to build a new pueblo and mission. This second church, dedicated to San Diego, was destroyed by unknown causes late in the 19th century. The church standing today was constructed in 1915.

Except on Feast Day, modern Tesuque holds little interest for most visitors. It is not an exceptionally friendly pueblo, and, except for a few pottery displays and the relatively new San Diego Mission, it ceased almost entirely except for poorly made "tourist pottery." Most of this was fired on top of kitchen stoves, if at all.

Recently, however, a few Tesuque potters have returned to more traditional methods, and they are now producing an exquisite black-and-red-on-white ware that is of excellent quality. A small amount of silver and turquoise jewelry is also made.

There are no shops or trading posts at Tesuque. The few artisans at the pueblo usually sell from their homes.

PUBLIC CEREMONIES   Dances and footraces are held in late May or early June, November, and during the Christmas period. Dates vary from year to year, so call the pueblo before your visit.

Tesuque Feast Day, dedicated to patron San Diego, occurs annually on November 12. The festivities are usually accompanied by the harvest dance.

Cameras, tape recorders, and sketch pads are strictly prohibited at all Tesuque ceremonies and will be confiscated if found.

VISITOR FACILITIES   Camel Rock Campground, an Indian-owned recreation site just north of the pueblo on U.S. 84–285, offers overnight camping and picnicking. RV sites, toilets, showers, drinking water, and a tribal store are available. Costs vary from year to year.

Telephone (505) 983-2667

holds virtually nothing for non-Indians to see or do.

About 300 people reside on the 17,000-acre reservation today. A few farmers still tend fields in the Tesuque River bottomland, but most working adults hold off-reservation jobs in Santa Fe or Los Alamos. In the past decade several dozen HUD homes were constructed on reservation land, and many of the younger adults prefer these to the crumbling adobe dwellings of the old village. The pueblo has no outside industry and takes little part in statewide Indian affairs.

Ceramic pitcher from Tesuque.
Right. Camel Rock.

The Pueblo of Zia

K E R E S A N

ORIGINAL INDIAN NAME   Tsiya—
meaning unknown.

HOW TO GET THERE   From Bernalillo, New Mexico, drive 19 miles
west on N.M. 44. The well-marked
entrance road is on the right.

ELEVATION   5,500 feet.

HOURS   8 A.M. to 5 P.M. except
during closed religious ceremonies.

ADMISSION   Free. As a courtesy
you should stop at the tribal
administration office near the
pueblo entrance to check in. Visits
to Our Lady of Assumption Mission are prohibited.

PHOTOGRAPHY   No. Cameras, tape
recorders, and sketch pads are forbidden on pueblo land.

INTERPRETIVE SERVICES   None. No
brochures available.

Zia pottery.

THE origins of Zia have been lost in time, but Spanish documents indicate the pueblo was one of 15 Keresan villages
occupied when Coronado arrived in New Mexico. García
López de Cárdenas was the first European to visit Zia in
1540. He was sent to the pueblo by Coronado to obtain hide cloaks for
the Spaniards so they would not freeze in the forthcoming winter.
Cárdenas reported that the village was whitewashed, and that many of
the thousand or so houses were trimmed in bright colors.

Juan de Oñate visited Zia in 1598 and estimated its population
at about 2,500. Shortly after his visit Spanish priests arrived and, using
forced Indian labor, began construction of a mission. In 1680 Zia revolted along with other pueblos in New Mexico, killing the resident
Spaniards and burning the church. Eight years later Domingo Cruzate,
temporary governor of New Mexico, led a heavily armed force up the
Río Grande in an attempt to retake the province. Cruzate met little
resistance during the first part of the trip, but at Zia he found 3,000
armed Indians protecting the village. Undismayed by the overwhelm-
ing numbers, Cruzate attacked. Two days later 50 Spaniards had been
wounded, but more than 600 Indians were dead and Zia was in flames.
Cruzate returned to El Paso with 70 prisoners, who were later sold as
slaves. Most of the battle's other survivors fled to the nearby
mountains.

When Diego de Vargas arrived, in 1692, Zia refugees had returned to the remains of their village. They quickly signed an oath of
obedience and, with Spanish help, rebuilt the pueblo and destroyed
mission. During the next few years Zia warriors assisted de Vargas in
several battles against other pueblos. According to some historians the
people of Zia are still considered social outcasts because of this early
friendliness toward the Spaniards.

ARTS AND CRAFTS   Zia potters are among the most talented of all pueblo artisans. Zia polychrome ceramics have always been in demand — by Indians and non-Indians alike — and very seldom does a substandard piece leave the pueblo. Typical Zia style is black, dark brown, and red on a pure white background. The best-known pottery design is the Zia bird, a long-legged, long-necked fellow, usually depicted with wings spread.

Little else in the way of arts and crafts is made at the pueblo. There are no trading posts or village shops. A few artisans sell from their homes (there are no signs; just knock on a door and ask for the nearest potter), but the best place to buy Zia pottery is one of the many pueblo Indian arts and crafts fairs held in the summer.

PUBLIC CEREMONIES   The only ceremony open to visitors at Zia is Our Lady of Assumption Feast Day, held annually on August 15. A corn dance usually accompanies the festivities. No cameras, tape recorders, or sketch pads are allowed.

VISITOR FACILITIES   None. Motel accommodations are available in Bernalillo.

Telephone (505) 867-3304

The Zia reservation consists of 112,000 acres. Inadequate water resources have greatly reduced agricultural projects at the pueblo, and most adults work off-reservation in Bernalillo or Albuquerque. Zia's present population is about 650.

The old village, perched atop a 300-foot-high lava-covered hill, has changed little since Spanish times. Most of the houses surrounding the original plaza exhibit little or no reconstruction work, and many are crumbling with time. Our Lady of Assumption Mission, located at the north end of the village, is the same one built in 1692. Below the old village are 40 new HUD homes in which many of the pueblo's younger inhabitants live.

Zia pottery.

The Pueblo of Zuni

The mission at Zuni.

ONCE thought by Spaniards to be the location of the fabled Seven Cities of Cíbola, Zuni offers the most detailed recorded history of all Southwestern pueblos. The Zuni people have probably occupied the region for at least a thousand years.

The first European to visit Zuni was Estevancio, a former Moorish slave (see *Introduction*) who, along with Spanish Fray Marcos de Niza, reached the Zuni village of Hawikuh (15 miles southwest of present-day Zuni) in 1539. Estevancio was killed by the Indians, but Fray Marcos returned to Mexico with tales of golden cities and treasure-laden streets.

The Coronado expedition reached Hawikuh in July 1540. Coronado was attacked but quickly took the offensive, capturing the village in less than an hour. He named the region Granada, but instead of seven golden cities he found six poor villages built of stone and mud. Coronado estimated the total population of the Granada pueblos at about 6,000.

The Spaniards occupied Granada from July 1540 to December, at which time Coronado led his expedition west to the Río Grande. After the conquistadors departed the villages were not visited again until 1580. Shortly after the second visit *Granada* was changed to *Zuni*, probably an adaptation of the Keresan word *sunyitsi*, the meaning of which is unknown. Juan de Oñate arrived in 1598, and with him came Spanish priests. In 1629 mission construction began at the two major Zuni towns of Hawikuh and Halona.

The Indians did not take well to Spanish religion, and in 1632 two priests were murdered by Zuni warriors. Fearing retaliation, the people abandoned their villages and fled to Thunder Mountain (now called Corn Mountain), a large mesa southeast of the pueblos. There

ters. Visitors are forbidden to photograph the kivas, masked dances, or any religious ceremonies or sacred areas. As a courtesy you should ask permission from individuals before taking their pictures.

Do not go near the Hepahteenah, a small hole covered with stones southwest of the village. This is the most sacred of all Zuni shrines. *Non-Indians are not welcome here.*

INTERPRETIVE SERVICES   Brochures that discuss pueblo history, local arts and crafts, and tribal fishing areas are available at tribal headquarters.

ARTS AND CRAFTS   Zuni artisans once produced a wide variety of fine arts and crafts but today are best known for their black-and-red-on-white animal-design pottery, and for silver jewelry decorated with turquoise, jet, and coral. Zuni jewelry, especially "needlepoint" (geometric designs formed with tiny bits of shaped turquoise and coral, then encased in silver), is considered by collectors to be the best of all pueblo handicrafts.

There are many arts and crafts shops in the village. A list of names and locations is available at tribal headquarters. Most are open seven days a week. The Zuni Trade Center and Zuni Craftsmen's Cooperative, both located on N.M. 53, probably offer the best prices.

PUBLIC CEREMONIES   Kachina dances (prayer dances to spirit ancestors described in the section *The Pueblos of the Hopi*) are held throughout the spring and summer they remained for three years, until coaxed back by a new set of priests.

In 1670 Apache raiders attacked Hawikuh, killed many of the residents, and burned the mission to the ground. The village was abandoned for good. Ten years later when the Pueblo Revolt occurred all of the Zuni fled once again to Thunder Mountain, and it was here in 1692 that Diego de Vargas found them. Without a skirmish the Zuni signed an oath of obedience and returned to the valley. Instead of reoccupying their old villages, however, they constructed a new one atop the site of old Halona, and it is this pueblo that stands today. A mission was erected along with the new village but was abandoned in the early 1800s. In 1968 it was rebuilt, and it is used by the villagers today.

The modern Pueblo of Zuni resembles the ancient villages of Shilwona not at all. Though a few of the old structures remain, they are well hidden by clusters of cut-stone houses, miles of telephone lines, and acres of tin roofs. Worse, adjacent to the old village is a new Zuni, a sprawling town of grocery stores, arts and crafts shops, gas stations, and new HUD houses. The abandoned ruins of Hawikuh, K'ianawa, Kwakina, Matsaki, and I'iakima (those of the sixth, Halona, being those occupied by the present Zuni Pueblo) have been left to crumble in the wind. They can be visited, but only with a guide.

Despite the movement toward modernization, tribal religion at Zuni is probably the strongest of any of the pueblos other than Hopi. Religious rites and secrets are jealously guarded, and most Zunis readily admit that, though they may attend church, white man's religion plays little role in their daily lives.

The Zuni reservation encompasses 406,000 acres, and tribal population is about 4,500. Farming and stock raising are important sources of income, but the massive arts and crafts industry (there are 900 silversmiths in the pueblo) and such seasonal work as firefighting and guiding big game hunters are responsible for a decrease in agricultural pursuits.

months at Zuni. Dates and times are variable and are usually unannounced; call the pueblo before your visit for up-to-date information.

Zuni has no feast day, but the Shalako Ceremonial, a year-long celebration of life, is one of the most beautiful and dramatic of all Indian religious ceremonies. The public portion of Shalako takes place in late November or early December. Exact dates are not set until October, so don't inquire until then. Cameras, tape recorders, and sketch pads are prohibited at all Zuni religious functions.

VISITOR FACILITIES   An RV campground located 3 miles east of the pueblo on N.M. 53 offers hookups, bathrooms, showers, drinking water, a dump station, and a grocery store. Sometimes, however, the campground is inexplicably closed. If you plan to camp, call first. The cost of camping permits varies.

Seven man-made fishing lakes on the Zuni reservation are open to the public. Anglers can catch northern pike, trout, bass, and catfish. Most of the lakes have primitive campgrounds nearby. Fishing permits cost $3 per day or $17 per season, and fishing is permitted 24 hours a day, year-round. Inquire at tribal headquarters for permits and current regulations.

Telephone (505) 782-4481

Zuni girl with needlepoint necklace and broach and cast belt buckle.

Calendar of Indian Dances and Ceremonies Open to the Public

January 23	San Ildefonso Pueblo	Feast Day
January	Most pueblos	Comanche, deer, and turtle dances and Three Kings Day ceremonies
	Hopi Pueblos	Various dances (including kachina)
February	Hopi Pueblos	Various dances (including kachina)
	Picurís Pueblo	Various dances
	San Felipe Pueblo	Buffalo dance
	San Juan Pueblo	Deer dance
	Santa Clara Pueblo	Various dances
	Taos Pueblo	Los Comanches dance
April	Most pueblos	Various dances
May 1	San Felipe Pueblo	Feast Day
May	Hopi Pueblos	Various dances (including kachina)
	Taos Pueblo	Footraces
June 13	Sandía Pueblo	Feast Day
June 24	San Juan Pueblo	Feast Day
June	Cóchiti Pueblo	Various dances
	Hopi Pueblos	Various dances and ceremonies (including kachina)
	Jemez Pueblo	Various dances
	Laguna Pueblo	Various dances
	San Felipe Pueblo	Various dances
	San Ildefonso Pueblo	Corn dance
	Santa Clara Pueblo	Buffalo and various other dances

	Santo Domingo Pueblo	Various dances
	Taos Pueblo	Corn and various dances
	Tesuque Pueblo	Corn dance
July 4	Nambé Pueblo	Nambé Falls Celebration
July 14	Cóchiti Pueblo	Feast Day
July	Hopi Pueblos	Various dances and ceremonies (including kachina)
	San Ildefonso Pueblo	Various dances
	San Juan Pueblo	Footraces, Indian arts and crafts show
	Taos Pueblo	Corn dance
August 4	Santo Domingo Pueblo	Feast Day
August 10	Picurís Pueblo	Feast Day
August 12	Santa Clara Pueblo	Feast Day
August 15	Zia Pueblo	Feast Day
August	All pueblos	Footraces
	Hopi Pueblos	Snake dances
	Jemez Pueblo	Pecos bull dance
	Laguna Pueblo	Corn dance
	Picurís Pueblo	Sunset dance

The church at Cóchiti circa 1899.

September 2	Acoma Pueblo	Feast Day
September 4	Isleta Pueblo	Feast Day
September 19	Laguna Pueblo	Feast Day
September 30	Taos Pueblo	Feast Day
September	Hopi Pueblos	Snake dance
	San Ildefonso Pueblo	Harvest dance
October 4	Nambé Pueblo	Feast Day
October	Hopi Pueblos	Various dances
November 12	Jemez Pueblo	Feast Day
	Tesuque Pueblo	Feast Day
November	Hopi Pueblos	Wuwutcimti (kachina) dance
December	Zuni Pueblo	Shalako Ceremonial
Christmas Period, December 23–25	Most pueblos	Various dances

List of Indian Pronunciations

Ácoma   AH-co-maw
Ákome   ah-co-MEY
Anasazi   an-na-SAW-zee
A'shiwi   ah-SHEE-wee
Astiolakwa   ah-stee-oh-LAH-kwa
Awatobi   ah-WAH-toe-bee
Bácobi   BAH-coe-bee
Cíbola   SEE-bow-lah (Spanish)
Cieneguilla   SEE-inna-GEE-ya (Spanish)
Cóchiti   COE-cha-tee
Guipui   goo-ee-POO-ee
Gyusiwa   gee-YOU-see-wah
Halona   hal-OHN-aw
Hano   haw-NO
Hapahteenah   haw-PAH-teen-ah
Hawikuh   HOW-wee-coo
Heishie   HEE-shee
Hopi   HO-pee
Hopituh   ho-PEE-two
Hótevilla   HO-te-vee-ya
I'iakima   aye-ee-ah-KEE-maw
Isleta   iss-LE-tah (Spanish)
Jemez   HAY-mess (Spanish)
Kachina   kuh-CHEE-naw
Katishtya   kaw-TEESH-taw-yaw
Kawaik   kaw-WAKE
Kawaiokuh   kaw-WHY-oh-koo
Keresan   CARE-uh-sahn
K'hapoo   ka-HAW-poo
K'ianawa   kay-EEAN-ah-wa

Kiva KEE-vah
Kotyete coat-yeh-TAY
Kwakina kwa-keen-NAW
Laguna lah-GOO-naw (Spanish)
Matsaki ma-tsaw-KEE
Mishongnovi mish-ONG-no-vee
Moenkopi mo-in-KOE-pee
Mojua-lua mo-haw-wah-LOO-wah
Naacnaiya naw-awk-nie-EE-yah
Nafiat naw-FEE-at
Nambé nam-BAY
Niman nee-MAN
Nuvatikiobi new-vah-TEE-kee-oh-bee
O'ke OH-kay
Oraibi oh-RYE-uh-bee
Oweenge oh-ween-JAY
Patoqua paw-TOE-quaw
Payupki pay-YUPE-kee
Perage pear-raw-JAY
Picurís pick-uh-REESE
Piwwetha pih-WAY-thaw
Po Pay po PAY
Powohgeonwige po-WAH-gee-own-wee-JAY
Pueblo PWEB-low (Spanish)
Puye poo-YAY
Sandía san-DEE-uh (Spanish)
San Felipe san fay-LEE-pay (Spanish)
San Ildefonso san ill-day-FON-so (Spanish)
San Juan san WAN (Spanish)
Santa Clara san-taw CLAIR-ah (Spanish)

Santo Domingo   san-toe doe-MING-go (Spanish)
Shilwona   sheel-WOE-naw
Shipaúlovi   shee-PAW-loe-vee
Shoshone   show-SHONE
Shungopovi   shun-go-PAW-vee
Sichomovi   see-cho-MOE-vee
Sunyitsi   sun-YEET-see
Taos   touse
Taugweaga   tog-wee-AH-gaw
Taytsoongay   tay-SOON-gay
Tesuque   tay-SOO-kay
Tewa   TEH-wah
Tiwa   TEE-wah
Towa   TOW-wah (ow as in cow)
Tsankawi   san-cow-WEE
Tsiya   TSEE-yah
Tua-tah   too-wah-TAH
Tusayan   too-saw-YAWN
Tyuonyi   chew-own-YEE
Uabunatota   ooh-AW-BOO-NAH-toe-tah
Walatow   wha-LAW-toe
Walpi   WALL-pee
Wuwutcimti   woo-woo-TSEEM-tee
Yugeuingge   ee-you-gee-you-EEN-gay
Zia   SEE-ah
Zuni   ZOO-nee

Capsule Guide to Indian Dances and Ceremonies

A Note about Indian Dances

THE origins of most Indian dances we see performed in the Southwestern pueblos today have long been lost in antiquity. There is no doubt, however, that the majority are centuries and perhaps millennia old.

Basically, Indian dances are a demonstration of gratitude — an offering of thanks to the traditional gods for the favors bestowed upon the pueblo, and a request that those favors continue. But to indicate that one dance means only this and another dance means only that would be an extremely incomplete description. Usually the dances non-Indians are privileged to watch are important but tiny parts of complex religious ceremonies that may last weeks or even continue through the year.

The dances listed here are those most likely to be seen being performed at the pueblos today. Remember, however, that the explanation provided with each dance is extremely general and meant to give the reader only a fundamental understanding of what is happening.

Basket Dance

Usually held in the spring, the basket dance offers a prayer to the gods for a successful planting season and an ample harvest. The basket itself symbolizes unplanted seed, the fruit or grain that the seed yields, and meal or flour that will eventually be made from the fruit.

Buffalo Dance

Bison were not common in the Southwest, but each winter most pueblos sent hunting expeditions east to search for the great herds. The buffalo dance ensured a successful hunt and also apologized to the bison for the killing that must soon occur. Traditionally it is a winter dance, but today it is often held during the summer for tourists.

Comanche Dance

Originating with the Plains Indians, the Comanche dance is a rite of manhood and celebrates courage in battle.

Corn Dance

The corn dance is part of the most important ceremony of the year for many pueblos. The dance is a request to the gods to provide adequate rainfall, quick growth for the crops, and a healthy, ample harvest. The Koshares—painted "delight makers" who cavort among the performers—serve two purposes: to instruct the dancers and to represent spiritual Indian ancestors.

Deer Dance

Deer, like buffalo, were once an important food source for Southwestern Indian tribes. The deer dance is an apology to the animals for the necessity of killing them, and also a request that they allow themselves to be slain easily by Indian hunters.

Eagle Dance

Masters of the sky, eagles were sacred to most pueblo tribes and were thought to have direct communication with the gods. The Eagle Ceremony asks the great birds, and consequently the sky spirits, for adequate rainfall. Primarily performed in spring, the eagle dance is often repeated during the hot summer months when rainfall is minimal.

Flute Dance

Performed by the Flute Society of the Hopi, the flute dance is a midsummer prayer ceremony requesting adequate rain for the crops.

Matachina Dance

The ceremony of the matachina dance originally was taught to the Indians of Mexico by Spanish priests. Though performed as a Christmas celebration today, the main characters are hardly Christians: They are Montezuma, once ruler of the Aztecs, and Malinche, an Indian interpreter for Hernán Cortés, the Spanish conquistador who conquered Mexico in 1521.

Snake Dance

Held only at the Hopi Mesas, the snake dance offers a prayer to the plumed water serpent and the gods of the underworld. It asks for adequate rainfall and a successful harvest.

Shalako Ceremonial

The Shalako Ceremonial, held only at Zuni Pueblo, is a year-long celebration of the continuance of life. It gives thanks to the Creator for His blessings and asks that those blessings continue. The public portion of the Shalako occurs in late November or early December.

For Further Reading

Abbot, Charles Greeley. *North American Indians.* New York: Smithsonian Institution, 1929.

Bahti, Tom. *Southwestern Indian Tribes.* Las Vegas: KC Publications, 1968.

Beck, Warren A. *New Mexico: A History of Four Centuries.* Norman, Okla.: University of Oklahoma Press, 1962.

Beck, Warren A. and Ynez D. Haase. *Historical Atlas of New Mexico.* Norman, Okla.: University of Oklahoma Press, 1969.

Bolton, Herbert Eugene. *Coronado: Knight of Pueblos and Plains.* Albuquerque: University of New Mexico Press, 1949.

Courlander, Harold. *The Fourth World of the Hopis.* New York: Crown Publishers, 1971.

Dutton, Bertha P. *Indians of the Southwest.* Santa Fe: Southwestern Association on Indian Affairs, 1965.

Forresť, Earle R. *Missions and Pueblos of the Old Southwest.* Chicago: Rio Grande Press, 1962.

Gibson, Michael. *The American Indian: From Colonial Times to the Present.* New York: Putnam's, 1974.

Glubok, Shirley. *The Art of Southwest Indians.* New York: Macmillan, 1971.

Horgan, Paul. *The Heroic Triad.* New York: Holt, 1970.

Hrdlicker, Ales. *The Coming of Man from Asia in the Light of Recent Discoveries.* Washington, D.C.: Smithsonian Institution, 1935.

Lavender, David. *The Southwest.* New York: Harper & Row, 1980.

Mays, Buddy. *Ancient Cities of the Southwest.* San Francisco: Chronicle Books, 1982.

National Geographic Society. *The World of the American Indian.* Washington, D.C.: National Geographic Society, 1974.

Reader's Digest. *America's Fascinating Indian Heritage*. Pleasantville, N.Y.: Reader's Digest Books, 1978.

Ritch, W. G. *New Mexico Blue Book*. Albuquerque: University of New Mexico Press, 1882.

Roberts, Frank Harold Hanna. *The New World Paleo-Indians*. Washington, D.C.: Smithsonian Institution, 1944.

Rothenberg, Jerome. *Shaking the Pumpkin*. Garden City, N.Y.: Doubleday, 1972.

Simmons, Marc. *Witchcraft in the Southwest*. Flagstaff, Ariz.: Northland Press, 1974.

Stewart, Dorothy N. *Handbook of Indian Dances*. Santa Fe: Museum of New Mexico, 1952.

Stubbs, Stanley A. *Bird's Eye View of the Pueblos*. Norman, Okla.: University of Oklahoma Press, 1962.

Terrell, John Upton. *Pueblos, Gods, and Spaniards*. New York: Dial Press, 1973.

Toulouse, Betty. *Pueblo Pottery of the New Mexico Indians*. Santa Fe: Museum of New Mexico, 1977.

Warner, John Anson. *The Life and Art of the North American Indian*. Los Angeles: Crescent Books, 1975.

Waters, Frank. *Book of the Hopi*. New York: Ballantine Books, 1963.

Zuni Pueblo elder.

Index